REBUILDIN

How the Game of Kubb
Put My Life Back Together

by Garrick van Buren

ISBN: 0-9862462-0-4
ISBN-13: 978-0986246203

Cover photo by Lynn Saegert

DEDICATION

To Jen, Cooper, Waverly, Augustus, and Penelope.

Thank you for continually inspiring me to get better at being a husband, better at being a father, and better at being me.

CONTENTS

Appendices

ACKNOWLEDGMENTS

Thank you:

> Kristin and Lewis Dijkstra and family for introducing me to kubb.
>
> My teammates on the Kubbchucks, Jamie Thingelstad and Jim Bernard, for finding the game as delightful as I do.
>
> Patrick Rhone for being a trusted sounding board throughout the writing of this book.
>
> Eric Maisel for the encouragement to write this story.

GARRICK VAN BUREN

PROLOGUE

On May 20, 2011, at 11:40 AM, Kristin
wrote:

> I was in the Scouts shop today, where
> they have tons of games and crafts
> equipment, and I came across a game
> called Kubb, "The Viking Game." It
> apparently originated in 13th century
> Sweden and is a cross between horseshoes
> and petanque or boules. I was intrigued
> and probably would have bought the set if
> it hadn't been a big, heavy bag of wood
> and if I hadn't already stopped at the
> discount book shop and bought more than I
> could carry home.
>
> Have you ever played this game? We
> might have to look into getting a
> set.
>
> Love, Kristin

1.
I'M NOT DOING SO WELL

The clock in my office flipped to 2:30 a.m..

At this hour, I'm breaking software faster than I'm fixing it. But, unless I completely bring the system down, I won't even notice until tomorrow—after you've signed in, expecting the website to work as it did yesterday. It's one thing to collapse into bed at 3 a.m. knowing I've made your tomorrow better —it's quite another knowing I've caused some small part of the internet to go dark. I know this because this wasn't the first time.

This was the second night this week. Maybe the third. Unfortunately, I wasn't an insomniac staring at the ceiling— there's lots of ways to treat insomnia. I was still in my office working. Sort of. Maybe. I was desperately fighting to get some internet technology I barely understood behave the way I wanted. This could have been a client project. But I doubt it—I likely stopped client work at 10 p.m.; 11 p.m. for sure. Whatever I'm working on, I'm one sleep-deprived keystroke from completely breaking everything I've done to this point. As I brush my teeth, too exhausted to actually feel disappointed at myself, I wonder, "Maybe, just maybe, I can get up and fix it before anyone notices. Before my three kids start demanding breakfast. Before the emails start rolling in asking what happened."

7 a.m. comes really fast when your head hit the pillow at 3am. On the good mornings, all three kids—all under five years old—would answer my selfish prayers to sleep an extra 30 minutes before pulling and tugging at my still exhausted body. On the bad days, one of them screams frantically from teething pain, a massively filled diaper, or because of this winter's common cold—just as I tuck myself in.

When my oldest child was still a baby in the crib, sometime between 6:30 and 7 a.m. he would fill his diaper so loudly it'd wake his mother and me. I'd get up to change him. As he grew older, he'd just yell for me: "Papa, Papa, Papa, Papa, Papa, Papa…" until I picked him out of his crib. Once he was in a bed, he'd get himself out of bed, toddle down the hall into my bedroom, work his way to my side of the bed, shouting "Breafkast Time!" smack in the middle of a rare REM cycle. In case I didn't immediately respond, his little sister was hanging in the shadows. Every morning at 7a.m..

From 7-9 a.m., I down my first pot of coffee while barking at my kids to stop making messes, to get dressed faster, to actually brush their teeth, all while I read email and over-reacted to the smallest inconvenience with more yelling. Then, if all was going according to schedule, I'd start my commute down the ten stairs into my basement home office. The same office I left six short hours ago. For the next hour, I'd drown myself in email, Facebook, and Twitter. By now, the rest of the family has left for school or the neighborhood gym, so I'd work my way up to the now quiet kitchen for a second pot of coffee.

Then back in front of the 30" computer monitor. I'd begin by fixing whatever I broke before my brain stopped working at 3 a.m. and slowly make progress on my actual To Do list. Most days, I'd just stare at the things on the list—too tired to even begin. I'd walk up the stairs and reheat some takeout leftovers for lunch. Then back down the stairs, letting the afternoon hours melt away just as I did the morning ones. Staring at the monitor. Finally, as if unchained, I'd leave my office at 5 p.m.. Not even caring I'd accomplished nothing. It was time to be a dad for the two hours between dinner and bedtime.

Rather than savor the bedtime routine, I'd burn through it as quickly as possible; changing the kids into pajamas at ludicrous speed followed by supersonic readings from their latest library book. As soon as the kids were in bed, back down the stairs I'd go.

This was my normal, my everyday. My daily exercise routine was up and down those stairs between the coffee maker and my computer. I'd forgotten the last time I'd shaved. I'd forgotten whether the clothes I was wearing were clean or just clean enough. Each time my dad would call—he'd ask, "When was the last time you went outside?"

I'd change the subject. I didn't know. I was self-destructing and didn't know how to stop.

Unfortunately, I was able to make this work.

Somehow.

Somehow I was able to keep enough clients happy to pay the mortgage, the grocery bills, the healthcare premiums, and contribute to the college funds. My marriage was still intact and I had three part-time employees. In fact, from a revenue perspective—this was by far my best year ever.

I knew I had a problem. I was convinced my problem was with my sleep. I was convinced the problem with my sleep was that I just didn't feel sleepy. So, I started taking 3mg of melatonin each night to just feel sleepy. For a couple months it worked—and I'd be drowsy and in bed around 11 p.m. every night. But bad habits die hard and I started to play chicken with the melatonin. I dared it to put me to sleep before its effects wore off. I built up a tolerance. Even though the drowsiness put me in bed by 11pm, I'd be wide awake staring at the ceiling 90 minutes later, debating whether or not I should head into my office. I upped the dose to 5mg—it just caused me to stare at the ceiling longer and with more alertness.

After the melatonin stopped working completely, I tried Universal Nutrition's ZMA (Zinc, Magnesium, and vitamin B6) Pro. The comments at Amazon and Universal Nutrition's own marketing copy praised it for providing a restful night's sleep. Exactly what I needed. Unfortunately, it instead caused my already hair-trigger temper to flair more frequently. In fewer than 30 days, my wife, Jen, demanded I stop taking it.

I switched to Vitamin D on the assumption that increasing my dosage of Vitamin D would simultaneously increase my naturally generated melatonin. It didn't. I gave up on supplements and went back to barley wine as my sleep aid.

At the time, I was building marketing websites for publicly-traded corporations and small businesses while playing around with interesting internet technologies on my own projects. This shouldn't be high stress. The failure state for these projects—missing deadlines, unresolved bugs, slower than ideal load times—are not a matter of life, death, or national security. None of the work was directly tied to my client's revenue growth. Nor was any of it my best work, or projects I was excited about. I wasn't even proud enough of my results to use any of it in my own marketing for my own business.

This work was destroying me. A voice deep inside of me yelled ever louder that at any moment—my business, my family, my house, my cars—will be completely taken away from me. Unless, of course, I work even harder. If I just worked a little harder, a little faster, held my breath just a little bit longer—everything would magically stabilize and I could exhale.

#

I spent the early years of my career in Chicago, bouncing from nascent web development agency to startup and back trying to say one step ahead of the dot com bust. In most places that was nine months, maybe a year. My longest stretch was 18 months. There were so many companies, with such short lifespans, the only consistency was me and the morning train ride into downtown Chicago. Jen and I were living within walking distance of both the L and the Metra, so depending on where I was going and when I needed to be there—I'd take one or the other. On this day, it was the L. The train car was completely empty in the middle of rush hour. Or at least, I remember being completely alone as I had this unexpected conversation with myself:

"I'm not doing so well."

"Have I felt this way before?"

"Yes."

"Lots of times?"

"More than a few."

"Do you think it'll get better?"

"Maybe. I don't know how. This feels pretty bad."

"Huh. Would changing jobs help?"

"Maybe. I guess that's doing something."

At which point the train arrived at my stop, and I'd need to focus on navigating my way to the office with the other commuters. I'd forget the entire conversation until the next quiet train ride when I was alone with thoughts. Despite the number of times I had this conversation with myself, I never told anyone and never explored it any further than starting the hunt for a new job.

That was before kids, before mortgages, back when both my wife, Jen, and I were bringing home paychecks. Today, it's up to me and my business to maintain the lifestyle we want for ourselves and our young family.

#

It's highly likely I've suffered from a low-grade, chronic depression for more than fifteen years. Maybe twenty. A depression that still allowed me to pay the bills and maintain a few relationships—even through the shocks of a major depressive episode. Like this episode. This episode that won't let me sleep.

2.
NO HELICOPTERS

I'm sure you're fortunate to have friends that have always been there for you. Friends that have continually shown you all the love, support, and generosity you should be granting yourself. Friends far closer to family than random people. My two oldest and dearest friends—Kristin & Lewis—are like that. It's no surprise I met them through my wife, decades ago. Before we were married. Before they were married. Today, they live half the world away and every summer we adjust our schedule so we can spend just one or two days with them.

In the summer of 2011, they brought with them 17 pieces of gorgeously stained maple. They said it was a fun, new game and proceeded to pound four stakes into the backyard and set five blocks on each short end of a rectangle, a larger 'king' piece in the middle of the entire rectangle. We took turns throwing the six batons underhand at the five blocks on the other side of the rectangle. We laughed at not being able to knock over the blocks. Delighted and undeterred, we continued throwing batons at these blocks. Again and again —they remained standing. It didn't matter, we played all weekend. Adults and kids together. The futility of throwing wooden sticks at wooden blocks 20 feet away was occasionally rewarded by the timeless, satisfying, and surprising 'thwack' when they met.

"Kubb" *(rhymes with "tube")* they called it, it was from somewhere in Scandinavia. They stumbled upon it in a games and crafts shop in Brussels—just a bag of wood on the floor below some pictures of very enthusiastic players.

They were unsure of the actual rules, if there were actual rules. That's fine. Rules usually feel arbitrary, overly-complicated, and overly-constricting. I'm as likely to misunderstand them as I am to forget them.

All that weekend I was outside in the sunshine with my kids, my wife, and my beloved friends throwing blocks of wood across the lawn. No internet, no electronics, no technological anything. Just primitive blocks of wood, grass, sun, and love. With each throw I felt closer to closer to my family, closer to nature, and closer to my Norwegian ancestry. I don't even care if this silly game has any rules. I'm giddy in love with its simplicity and its utter lack of modern technology.

I've never been to Scandinavia. My Norwegian ancestors immigrated to the United States more than 110 years ago. Until my introduction to kubb, I'd never pondered daily life among the fjords, glaciers, and mountains on the northwestern coast of Norway in the 1800s. Yet, these primitive blocks transported me to:

- a clearing in a Scandinavian forest where a dad, after collecting enough firewood for the winter smiles as he chops off a few more branches and squares up a few extra logs as a kubb set for his children's Christmas gift.

- a beach along the cold Norwegian Sea where a group of sailors are passing the time playing kubb as they await their next trade journey.

- the front yard of a mountain farmstead, where young neighboring families are playing kubb and laughing together under cloudless skies after cleaning up from dinner.

With each baton I threw, another Nordic vision passed though my mind. Each vision more romantic, more comforting, more rural, more domestic, and filled with more community and generosity than the last.

Unfortunately, however, as all good things do, it came to an end. The next day, my friends continued on their American journey—and with them went kubb.

I retreated to the basement and restarted my downward spiral.

Yet, the game and the romantic visions haunted me.

A few weeks later, Jen got tired of me longing for kubb and purchased the Bex kubb set off Amazon. The pieces were shaped differently than the handmade maple set. The pieces, while still rectangular were smaller, narrower, lighter, with rounded edges. The box, covered in Viking iconography, promoted the game being centuries old. It sat unopened in the back corner of my office for months, whispering to me day in and day out. Then, in the middle of that slow-moving, unstructured week between Christmas and New Years—I opened the box. Immediately, spontaneously, uncharacteristically, I invited a dozen friends and neighbors over to play kubb in the uncharacteristically warm Minnesota winter.

Play we did.

We laughed at how deceptively difficult it was for any of us to topple a small block of wood with a baton. Doubly so when the only available light was the motion-triggered lamp on the garage or headlights from the occasional passing car.

We joked about taking this silly wooden game seriously.

We joked about making team shirts.

We joked about playing competitively.

We played and joked well into the morning hours.

As I finished cleaning up, the kitchen clock flipped to 2:30 a.m..

#

I started spending evenings scouring the internet for all things kubb.

Results were thin, inconsistent, and seemingly forgotten by their original publishers. Emails sent requesting more information were unanswered.

Then, somewhere into day three or four, I found the registration page for the City of Lakes Loppet Foundation's Winter Kubb Tournament. The tournament was held outside in February in Minnesota as part of the Loppet Foundation's larger Nordic winter activity festival. A tournament? In town? In a few weeks?

A nervous, prickly, anxious, unbelieving enthusiasm flooded

over me. I was barely able to type out the email asking my friends Jim and Jamie to join me. Their replies came back immediately and as enthusiastically. I registered. I felt there must be something I should do in preparation. I had no idea what that would be. The idea of practicing—on my own or as a team—didn't even cross my mind. What would "practicing" even mean?

One Saturday, a few weeks later, I followed the comforting "thwack" of wood-hitting-wood across the parking lot through a line of trees into a clearing filled with the 16 kubb pitches of the Loppet Kubb Tournament. Many of them in use by teams that knew what they were doing. As we pass by one warm-up game, I scanned the arrangement of the blocks and I say, "Jim, there's this one part of the gameplay I don't understand." Jim shrugs as we wait for Jamie to arrive and the tournament to begin.

Even though it was early Saturday morning, I had already resolved a small client issue and was haunted by the anxiety of being across town from my office for another six hours. Then, from atop the ricketiest homemade platform, Eric Goplin, the tournament organizer stands over the 32 teams, and confirms we'll be playing by U.S. National Kubb Championship rules. From the audience, a player shouts a question about throwing the baton. Eric thanks the player and mocks throwing the baton underhand then lifts it up and holds it towards the audience while pivoting the baton from vertical to 10 degrees, showing that throws more than 10 degrees off vertical are illegal throws.

"Underhand only. No helicopters."

Helicopters and other angles weren't even part of the gameplay I had a question about. In fact, those questions didn't even cross my mind. What else don't I know?

My anxiety continues to rise. I'm feeling naked, awkward,

unprepared and completely outside my comfort zone. I fight a strong urge to run back to the car and drive home before the tournament even begins.

My questions about the gameplay were quickly answered once we started playing our first match. A helpful team, whose name is lost to history, guided us through the key aspects of the ruleset. I'm sure they easily won the match. It wasn't until after this forgettable match that I was exposed to kubb's true nature.

As we walk to start our second game, a young woman bundled in winter active wear pulls down her scarf and warns: "The team you're about to play—they don't ever miss."

We acknowledged the comment, but didn't know enough about kubb to know what it meant.

Our new opponent introduced themselves as Chad Bevers and Chad Parsons—playing as the Kubb Snipers from Fox Valley Kubb in Wisconsin. They were fast and accurate with a distinctive throwing style. While many teams split the batons evenly among the players with each player throwing all their allotted batons in their turn, the Kubb Snipers didn't. Each Chad threw two batons, then stepped back for the other Chad to throw their third baton.

Our first game with the Kubb Snipers lasted no more than five minutes. As did the second. Even so, this brief 2-0 match with the Kubb Snipers gave Jim, Jamie and me a glimpse of the strategy permeating the game, the bowling-esque short game it creates, the skill of throwing the wooden blocks into a pile, and the strategic contemplation required to the effectively tip them up defensively.

Our next match was with a far more casual team—a team more interested in the novelty of playing a goofy lawn game in the snow than showcasing their competitive skills. Or, that's what I inferred by their matching beanies complete with horns, mustache, beard, and ponytail.

We tried to quickly apply what we were learning. We clawed our way into the championship bracket. Once there, we were promptly eliminated. Exhausted, we returned to our families.

In the dark of a winter afternoon, the Kubb Snipers won the entire tournament.

#

After that tournament, I set up the 8-meter by 5-meter pitch in my backyard and practiced everything I knew. The 8-meter shots, throwing in the kubbs at four meters, raising them defensively, attempting to topple multiples with a single baton. I started spending hours outside, eking every last ray of winter's daylight. When I had a hard problem on a client project—I'd step outside and throw some kubb. I started sleeping better. I stopped drinking two pounds of coffee a week. My in-laws started commenting on how much more color was in my complexion.

Of course, our next tournament needed to be the 2012 US National Kubb Championship in Eau Claire, Wisconsin. For the next five months Jim, Jamie, and I played US National Kubb Championship over the noon hour in downtown Minneapolis. I joined the Minnesota Kubb club for Monday "friendlies"—non-competitive games—organized by the same Eric Goplin that organized the Loppet tournament. Every week I'd sheepishly step into the park again feeling awkward, green, vulnerable, and out of place. Every week I'd happily be the one in a two verses one match—simply to take as many throws as possible. Each week I'd leave the park winless and hungry to get better.

I was confident that six months of playing an obscure wooden lawn game on a weekly basis would sufficiently prepare us for the US National Kubb Championship. The competition couldn't be that much more experienced.

I was wrong.

I was overwhelmed by the intensity and talent of the teams. Seventy-six teams from the far corners of Iowa, Minnesota, Wisconsin, and Illinois were competing, not for money, but for a shot at getting their name on the Stapp King, USA Kubb's 1-meter tall, nine kilogram Championship trophy. Last year's winners, Team Knockerheads—from Des Moines, Iowa—wanted their name listed on the Stapp King twice.

Jim, Jamie, and me, the Kubbchucks, went ice cold. 8 meters, 4 meters, it didn't matter. We couldn't hit anything, but we could hold on. We'd get some lucky shots and be thankful for our opponents' unfortunate misses. If we didn't lose immediately, we could drag the game on for an hour. We'd create a slow painful grind only relieved by the tournament organizer calling time. Just like at the Loppet tournament— we clawed our way into the Championship bracket. Again, once there, we lost immediately.

Two long days in the humid, unrelenting heat of the Midwestern sun. I was exhausted and disappointed. I felt the Kubbchucks should have done better. I felt I should have done better. After I returned home—I didn't touch my kubb set for a week. My mind was struggling to reconcile the canyon between my perceived ability and my actual performance against those more experienced players.

My honeymoon with kubb was now over. My marriage to kubb was just beginning.

#

While there are a number of variations in backyard kubb gameplay, competitive kubb is played under the World Championship rules (vmkubb.com) or the US National Kubb Championship rules (usakubb.org). If you've not played before, or not played under the competitive rulesets, the key aspects of the competitive gameplay are:

- Five kubbs (each kubb measuring 15 cm tall by 7 cm square) are placed evenly on each 5-meter side of a 5-meter by 8-meter rectangular outline.

- The king (measuring 30 cm tall by 9 cm square) is placed directly in the middle of the rectangle.

- To determine which team goes first—on the count of three, one player from each team tosses one baton underhand at the king. The team with the baton closest to the king—without knocking it over—can chose to start the game or to select which side they'd like.

- The teams then take turns tossing six batons at the opposing side's five baseline kubbs attempting to topple them.

- After the sixth baton has been thrown, the opposing team gathers up all the batons and toppled kubbs.

- The opposing team then begins their turn by throwing the toppled kubbs back onto the pitch, at least halfway (past the king).

- These field kubbs are then stood up—as if on a hinge—by the non-throwing team. *(This was the part I didn't understand as I walked into my first tournament).*

3
THROW ONE BATON

It doesn't matter which ruleset we're playing by, which tournament we're in, or the size of our team—kubb is played one baton at a time. That one baton's sole job is to topple a field kubb, a base kubb, or the king. Under the right circumstances it will topple them consistently and accurately.

For me accuracy starts with removing all other thoughts from my head. Clearing my mind and focusing completely on the bottom of the target kubb topples it every time. Always. Any single other thought guarantees a miss. Always. That single thought could be; a client issue, a disagreement with my wife that I didn't handle well, or how this baton throw could win the game. Even the hesitation and self-doubt over whether this is the kubb I should be targeting. Once that other thought sneaks in, I'll miss. Guaranteed.

I found the most effective way to eliminate all other thoughts is to flip the baton counting to six or ten before I throw it. With each flip; I focus my mind on the target kubb, I confirm my body's approach, I confirm my location on the pitch, I appreciate the weight of the baton, and confirm my grip. When I reach the final number, whatever number it is, the rest of the world has melted away—it's just me, the baton, and a single target kubb. I'm no longer thinking, only trusting. I'm trusting my body is in the most comfortable, successful position. I'm trusting my mind to only be aware of the baton, the targeted kubb, and how to connect them.

Just as a tennis player counts out bounces of the tennis ball before a serve, or a basketball player counts out bounces of the basketball before a free-throw—counting baton flips is my pre-throw routine. A routine preparing both the mind and the body to perform at a high level consistently.

#

In the spring of 2012, midway between the Loppet and the US Kubb National Championship, my focus, accuracy, and consistency on the kubb pitch had increased substantially. I wanted those same improvements off the pitch. That meant finally establishing a regular meditation practice. Up until that point, every time I had attempted to sit and focus on my breath, my anxious monkey brain ego would get the best of me. I'd immediately jump up and execute on whatever ridiculously small thing it thought was more important. The moment my body would settle, my mind would demand I keep going by immediately reminding me of the million tiny things my previous task was holding at bay.

In the opening chapter of *"The Willpower Instinct"*, Kelly McGonigal Ph. D. at Stanford, argues mindful meditation is exercise. Sitting quietly, placing our attention on the circle of our breath, then gently returning attention to our breath when our mind wanders—this simple act practiced by so many for hundreds of years, is exercise. Exercise for the frontal lobe—the part of our brain responsible for long-term decision making, focus, and sustained willpower.

One cool spring weekend, Jen and I drove to a small, newly opened resort on Lake Superior's north shore. Jen's goal—train for a half marathon. My goal—meditate. I brought no electronics, no cameras, no books, no client work. While Jen went on hours-long runs, it was just me and nature's stillness. Nothing for me to do except echo the stillness back. Within the stillness of these three days, every weakness, insecurity, and vulnerability buried deep in my psyche surfaced like so many hideous leviathans:

- Heartbreaking feelings of abandonment and personal worthlessness following my parents' divorce twenty years prior.

- Deep-seeded memories of detachment, isolation, and naive faux pax in a foreign country while on a student exchange ten years prior.

- A haunting sense that persistent self-sabotage caused me to lose so many of the professional opportunities I pursued.

- Agony that this self-sabotage was perpetuating these self-defeating feelings of isolation and inadequacy.

- Pain that I'm not actually as capable, not as effective, not as talented, as I believed I was.

- A nausea-inducing thought that these dark emotions, as old and deep as they were, were just below the surface of my consciousness.

- The irony that I'm alone in this darkened room struggling with feelings of isolation.

My only responsibility and my only ability was to acknowledge these dark sea monsters directly and honestly then refocus my attention on my breath. No reaction, just acknowledge and refocus. Acknowledge and refocus. Sometimes refocusing required counting my breaths just as I would count baton flips.

Each meditation session felt like it lasted hours. In reality it was only 20 minutes. Or 17 minutes. Or 23 minutes. After which I'd stand up, emotionally and mentally exhausted, and eat a small bite. Then I'd walk one of the trails appreciating the stoic persistence of the trees and the vastness of Lake Superior. Then I'd return to the cabin and sit again. This was easily the most sobering and emotionally-challenging two days I'd ever experienced. And it was just me.

Once I returned to civilization, my daily meditation practice became much easier to adopt. Usually, a single 20-minute session before breakfast would serve me the entire day. On difficult days, when I again felt overwhelmed and the frazzled monkey brain ego was creeping back—I'd sit for another 20 minutes. While meditation doesn't help me solve problems—it does help me return my focus to my key targets, allowing everything else to melt away. Sometimes, when I sit, the quiet, vast, stillness comes quickly. Other times I'd spend 20 minutes counting exhales unsuccessful in pulling my attention from some especially compelling thought.

In kubb, as in meditation, my accuracy increased dramatically when I started building my throws atop my breath. Whether a baton throw or kubb throw—I get my body in the throwing position, take a deep inhale as I pull my arm back and then time my exhale to the exact moment

24

the baton leaves my hand. From acting to powerlifting to running to kubb to meditation, breath is the foundation of all other activities. A misaligned breath easily holds back performance. When I'm paying attention to my breath, I'm paying attention to my mind, which means I'm paying attention to the task at hand. Without breath and mind aligned, the body will never be.

#

I now have four children, as I write this the youngest still in diapers. There have been times when juggling their simultaneous needs has taken me to the point of frazzled frustration. This isn't unusual for parents of fewer than four kids or those with more than four. I've found that four is the maximum number of simultaneous requests my brain can support before getting confused, overloaded, and I start making boneheaded mistakes. After enough boneheaded mistakes, I now make a deliberate effort to commit to one thing at a time, and focus on completing it to the best of my ability.

Like digital bandwidth and lanes on the freeway, our organic brains have only so much bandwidth, the greater traffic volume the slower and less reliably it moves. The truth is, nothing in your life actually needs to happen simultaneously, right now. That requirement is self-imposed and more about external signaling (e.g. "I'm so busy the only time I can talk to you is while I'm driving") at the expense being fully present. Things can happen sequentially, asynchronously, and some time later, usually with no downsize. If they respect you, people can wait a minute until you've reached a stopping point and can commit your full attention.

Outside a family function last year, I saw an extended relative talking on their phone while juggling a cigarette and a beer in the other hand. I was struck by how many things he was doing simultaneously—attending a family function, smoking a cigarette, talking on the phone, and drinking a beer. Many of them marketed to bring us closer together. How many he had actually committed to? None.

At home, Jen and I will remind each other to "Do One Thing" when it looks like one of us is inadvertently and unnecessarily multi-tasking. "Do One Thing" a gentle reminder to re-commit and complete the one thing we're doing rather than slowing down the completion by introducing a new, completely different thing. We could be making dinner while going through the mail or cleaning up a mess one of the kids made while on hold with the bank. Looking up something on the internet while attempting to maintain a conversation. One of those things can always wait one more minute.

Next time you're driving, look for the distracted drivers. It's not difficult. They're the cars that seem just out of the regular flow of traffic; the car that won't get out of your blind spot, the one that won't let you safely merge or cross lanes. The driver in that car is quite likely attempting to maintain a conversation on the phone and they're doing so just as poorly as they're driving.

For me, multi-tasking was largely about comforting my need to be wanted; not wanting to miss out, wanting to appear capable—often at a super-hero level. Unfortunately, my inability to prioritize and commit to one thing at a time meant I was constantly missing out, wasn't ever working on the most important things, and always appeared distracted, rattled, and inept. Self-sabotage at its best.

Shortly after my second child, Waverly, was born, my mother-in-law stayed with us for a few days to help out. One afternoon, I met her and my oldest child—two-and-a-half at the time—slowly returning home from a walk around the block. They'd been gone more than an hour—stopping at every spray-painted line on the curb marking a gas, water, or electricity line. The toddler demanded each color required a different kind of jump. My frazzled, sleep-deprived brain, frustrated at being unable to focus on professional concerns, nearly exploded at the tediousness they described. I asked her how she managed it:

"This is what I'm doing," she replied.

Her combination of nonchalance, commitment, confidence, and straight-forwardness in describing the slowest possible walk around the block stunned me. She was absolutely right, there was nothing more important to do. Even as slowly as my brain was working I understood. I was frazzled and frustrated because I was multi-tasking. Even without the sleep-deprivation a newborn brings, I was worried, anxious, and insecure, trying to minimize multiple potential negative outcomes in my personal and professional lives. Turns out, the only answer is not doing more things, but doing fewer. Doing just one thing at a time. Especially when it's spending an hour outside in the sunshine exploring the world through a toddler's eyes.

#

No matter the size, each team only has six baton throws per turn. Whether you're throwing or your opponent is—it's tempting to count the remaining batons after each throw. It's tempting to hold onto the memory of a momentum-changing shot. It's tempting to set aside a baton for the king shot before the first baton is thrown. Don't. Kubb is too dynamic a game, every baton—hit or miss—changes the strategy for both sides of the pitch. The only baton to focus on is the one in your hand, the one you're about to throw. All the other batons are ancient history or an unknowable future. Only the one baton in your hand is controllable. Commit to connecting this one baton and its one target.

Back in the 2012 US National Kubb Championship, the Kubbchucks were deep in a match with an equally skilled team, The Engineers. In the middle of the second game we were at a stalemate. Seven field kubbs were in play with no forward progress by either team. They'd throw in seven, they'd topple seven. I'd throw in seven, we'd topple seven. Back and forth, forth and back. Six batons toppling seven kubbs. The heat of mid-July's noon sun was wearing me down. I was exhausted and reeked of dirt, sweat, and sunscreen. I started talking to myself:

"What am I doing?"

"Throwing in seven kubbs."

"How long have I been throwing in seven kubbs? Always?"

"It doesn't matter, it's what I'm doing right now. Commit to now. Commit to throwing in these seven to the best of your ability."

This commitment in the midst of a malaise improved the placement of the field kubb just enough. Just enough for us to clear the seven field kubbs with five batons instead of six. Leaving one baton to be thrown. As Eric Anderson, the tournament organizer, walked over to call our match on time, I aligned my breath, focused on my target, and threw the one baton toppling one more baseline kubb.

The Kubbchucks advanced to the Championship bracket. The throwing team must first topple these field kubbs before attempting to topple any kubbs standing on the 5-meter baseline.

This pattern continues back and forth until one team topples all five baseline kubbs and the king.

Within this simple, rhythmic gameplay lay a struggle for

accuracy, a universe of strategic thinking, and the need to best your toughest opponent—yourself.

4.
BUILD A CITY

Football has a Quarterback, curling has a Skip, and baseball has a Catcher. Each of these roles are responsible to be aware of the game state, the conditions of the playing field, and leading their team to success through all the potential outcomes. In kubb this position is the Inkastare (roughly translated "one who throws in"). The Inkastare's primary role in kubb is to strategically throw the kubbs into a dense cluster to be toppled with the fewest number of batons possible. Once all the kubbs have been thrown in ("inkast"), the defending team tips them up. Once the defending team has left the pitch, the throwing team, Inkastare included, demolish the cluster of kubbs, like monsters in a tokusatsu movie.

I am the Kubbchucks Inkastare. Jim, in addition to being a Blaster—equivalent to a batter in baseball—on the

Kubbchucks, is also the catcher on the legendary softball team he manages. Jim knows the value of ensuring the Pitcher is in the right headspace. In that match with The Engineers for the Championship bracket, each time I prepared to throw in seven kubbs, as sweat dripped off my forehead onto my glasses, Jim calmly requested: "Garrick, build me a city."

"Build me a city."

Cities broadly speaking are dense constructs of wood, steel, and concrete snug against a natural boundary—an ocean, a lake, a river, a mountain. Filled with unknowable complexity and continually re-arranged to make daily life easier and more enjoyable for thousands of people.

Twenty years after it was originally published, I discovered architect Christopher Alexander's classic work, *"A Pattern Language"*. The 1200-page tome describes a Russian-nesting-doll-like generative grammar to construct the world around us in a sustainable and humane way;

- **'Connected Play'** describes a neighborhood connected to allow children to play easily and safely together.

- **'Quiet Backs'** describes the need for a quiet, natural setting behind buildings to encourage us to pause and refresh ourselves.

- **'Scattered Work'** describes the need to zone for multiple concentrations of workplaces throughout a city to minimize the separation between our home and work lives.

In all *"A Pattern Language"* describes 253 patterns and, nearly 40 years after its first publishing, remains a well-referenced volume by practicing urban planners.

Throughout *"A Pattern Language"* and all of Alexander's work is the reminder that architecture—whether homes, neighborhoods, or cities—creates spaces for people.

Similarly a good Inkastare knows they are architecting a space. Architecting a space with kubb, not for them, but for their Blasters. Just as architecture is not complete until people move about it—the inkast is not complete until the kubbs are raised and batons start flying. As such, throwing in kubbs also has generative patterns—starting points for architecting a turn. Last winter, when the double digit below zero wind chill kept me from playing kubb outside, I spent nights on the living room floor arranging, raising, and re-arranging ten kubbs searching for the most offensively optimal arrangement. Then I worked backwards to the inkast. From that, I've developed a framework for inkasting kubbs in all scenarios:

1 Kubb
If you're feeling conservative land it just in front of the centerline—so it's just 50% in bounds when tipped up. Yes, that place where it didn't actually land in bounds, but it can be tipped up in bounds, that's where you want it. This creates the shortest possible throw.

 If you're feeling confident and want to send a clear competitive message throw the kubb directly in front of your favorite baseline kubb. Topple this single field kubb with a single baton and you're no worse off then if it was short. But, topple the field kubb and base kubb with a single baton and you've just shifted the momentum of the game in your favor.

2 Kubbs
Land these two so they'll tip up as close to each other as possible. Based on my research the most reliable way to do this is to land the first one atop the sideline and parallel with the centerline then land the second one perpendicular to

the first—forming a "T". But really, it doesn't matter if they land side-by-side or front-to-back, the key is to topple them both with the first baton leaving five batons for the baseline kubbs.

3 Kubbs
Land all three straddling the sideline just behind the center pin, like three horizontal stripes parallel to the center line. Straddling the sideline means the defending team has no choice but to raise them near each other. This formation makes toppling three kubbs with a single baton as straight-forward as two kubbs.

If these three field kubbs are from your baseline—you should be able to close the game out in four batons. If they're your opponent's, you can still make a solid dent in your own baseline kubbs once you clear these field kubbs. Do it quickly. If you're feeling bold—land all three kubbs on the same side of the pitch as your remaining base kubbs and send enough power through the field kubbs to make them (and your baton) topple some base kubbs.

If you're feeling conservative—just knock down the three field kubbs with a single baton and move on.

4 Kubbs
Make two doubles just as described in the "2 Kubb" section. Estimate two batons to topple the four, aim for just one. In almost all scenarios the throwing team can close the game here or at least tie it up. Both teams should be prepared for a pivotal turn.

5 Kubbs
Now it gets interesting. One team has pulled ahead on baseline kubbs—or is completely dominating the game. Doubles are easier to hit than singles (two kubbs create a bigger target), so pair up the kubbs. Where does that leave the fifth kubb? The conservative strategy is to land two pairs

near the centerline and then throw one in front of a baseline kubb. The aggressive strategy drops all five kubbs right in the corner next to the center pin, and trusts the team to topple all the field kubbs with two batons or fewer.

If you've cleared your baseline, take a breath, and acknowledge that you can win the game with one baton per target. If your opponent's baseline is the one that's clear— the conservative strategy is the most defensive.

6 Kubbs
Statistically this is where teams, even high-performing teams, frequently leave a field kubb standing. Pair the kubbs up into three easy doubles. The conservative strategy is to make three distinct pairings—don't worry if they're near each other. Maybe even put one of those pairings at 6 meters or deeper. The aggressive strategy drops six field kubbs in the corner.

If you have any baseline kubbs remaining ignore them completely, they are only a distraction at this point. From this point on, simply clearing the field kubbs is success, for it immediately requires your opponent to do the same. This begins a battle of attrition.

7 Kubbs
Make two clusters, one of four and one of three. Estimate three batons (triple, double, double), hope for two batons (quad, triple). If you need to rethrow a kubb and you have base kubbs remaining—rethrow it at least 6 meters.

8 Kubbs
Build me a city. Dense as can be. Drop eight right next to the center pin, pair them up as best you can. No matter how well they're paired up, there's just so many kubbs that the toppled ones easily get in-between standing ones. This makes counting on four doubles risky. If your side has the two baseline kubbs remaining, averaging two field kubbs

per baton leaves you a baton for each of your baselines. Although, the primary goal is still to clear the field.

9 Kubbs

If it's your baseline kubb that remains—build a city next to the center pin on the same side of the pitch as the remaining baseline kubb. If it's been a clean inkast without any penalty kubbs or bizarre offshoots, then land number nine right in front of the remaining base kubb. This will create five groups of two. Even with a remaining baseline kubb, you could win the game here—provided the first five batons topple at least two kubbs each (which is why they're paired up). If there is a penalty kubb or a lonely kubb somewhere else on the pitch, consider it the deep kubb and drop the ninth in the woodpile.

If your opponent's baseline remains and it's been a clean inkast then drop the ninth kubb just behind the woodpile— where it could still be toppled easily by another kubb but would not provide a four meter advantage line to your opponent if it was missed. If there are penalty kubbs or other bizarre offshoots—again, throw number nine in the woodpile, take a deep breath, and get to work.

10 Kubbs
Now we've got a kubb game!

Ten field kubbs means all the kubbs are in play and no base kubbs remain to provide direction to the Inkastare. The only landmark is the king. Throw five solid doubles. That will give your team more than enough opportunity to win the game.

#

My preferred position to inkast is standing on the left side of the pitch, throwing with my left hand, so the kubbs are initially landing out of bounds then rolling in bounds—left to right. When done successfully, this creates a dense city that can be easily toppled by my right-handed teammates. When I'm not able to roll the kubbs in bounds, I scoot inside the pitch a little and throw just in front or behind the woodpile wherever I have the most space. I've thrown many a penalty kubb simply because I thought a few more inches existed between the centerline and woodpile.

The kubb pitch is as dynamic as the baseball diamond. The game changes after each kubb inkast and after each baton thrown. A team that takes the time to develop a framework and shorthand for communicating the changing pitch conditions will work stronger and more effectively on the pitch. They'll always be on the offense—no matter if they're throwing or not.

In baseball, the pitcher and the catcher have a strong relationship. They communicate with each other with each pitch, each batter, each change of the field conditions. The catcher's primary tool is throwing off the batter's mental game. The pitcher's primary tool is providing a pitch that looks just good enough to hit—but isn't. Together they're bound by a common goal to strike the batter out—or at least minimize runs batted in. They're conspiring, defensive players. In kubb, a similar relationship exists between the Inkstare and the First Blaster. Yet, unlike in baseball, this is an offensive relationship. The Inkastare needs to land the kubbs in a formation where the First Blaster can topple them all with a single baton. This requires communication and honesty. Honesty on where the Inkastare can land the kubbs and honesty on where First Blaster is confident in toppling them.

As an Inkastare, I like to stop inkasting after four kubbs and review how kubbs are landing with the rest of my team. With fewer than four there's less value in this mid-inkast review because there's a far lower chance of not being able to clear the field with six batons. Even with fewer than four field kubbs, a quick review of the pitch after each kubb is tossed is valuable—if only to develop a habit of communicating.

At the 2014 US National Kubb Championship, whenever I had more than three kubbs to throw, the Kubbchucks First Blaster, Jamie would stand at the center line while I inkast. After each kubb, he'd tell me whether it landed in or out, how much space I had to the center line, and where his ideal position for the next kubb was. We'd discuss where any rethrown kubbs should go. Jamie called it "directing traffic." As the team's Inkastare, this level of communication was unequivocally beneficial. Even though I had some unfortunate bounces, Jamie accurately telling me the state of the woodpile and clarifying the next target was like having another pair of eyes a few seconds into the future. It proved that inkasting is a two person job. Inkastare/blaster. Pitcher/catcher.

Just as the pitcher's job is to control the ball all the way to the catcher's mitt, the Inkastare's job is to control the kubb until it's toppled by a baton. The throwing technique that controls how a wooden rectangular prism flies through the air, where it lands, and where it comes to a stop is called "The Drill."

The key to The Drill is throwing the kubb underhand so that it flies at an angle and spins like a football in a downward spiral, or a drill bit. To get this controlled spin, I hold the back half of the kubb in my throwing hand between my thumb and index finger then hook the second knuckle of my middle finger around an edge of the kubb. When I release the kubb, my middle finger creates the spiral while my arm and wrist create the throwing arc. In ideal pitch conditions— a strong, healthy, soccer turf—a 30-degree angle should cause the kubb to land, stick, and maybe jump straight back an inch, before completely stopping. Lighter kubbs at a lower angle perform similarly. A lower angle also works better on softer terrains, like snow pack and sand, or for shoving kubbs tighter together by throwing them into one another head on. Steeper angles will cause the kubb to roll end-over-end before stopping well beyond where it landed.

Knowing how the kubbs will behave when thrown at different angles increases your ability to strategically roll the kubbs tighter together, filling in holes in the woodpile. In addition, to throw kubbs into each other or have them roll end-over-end, one of the most powerful methods of building a city is getting the kubbs to roll side-to-side after landing. Rather than landing straight on, to get a kubb to roll side-to-side after landing it needs to fly and land at an angle. The direction the top of the kubb is pointing—relative to the bottom—is the direction the kubb will roll, or cut, upon landing.

#

A successful Inkastare continually brings a large number of small elements into alignment. Everything from the position of their body, angle of their arm when throwing, the angle of the kubb when thrown, and the direction the kubb faces when it stops. Just as urban planners adjust and align small elements of our environment to encourage and discourage different behavior, the Inkastare aligns all of these small elements to influence how the kubbs are raised, and ultimately how many batons are required to topple them.

If my inkast goes as intended, it won't be for me. Jamie or Jim will completely clear it before I throw. In our daily lives, we don't have complete control over the actions of others. Not our partners, not our children, not our neighbors, not our direct reports, not our clients. Not even our teammates. We can however, do our part to set them up for success.

#

I went to college to be a graphic designer. Throughout my

studies I was encouraged to select color intentionally, to place type deliberately, and to have a meaningful reason for every decision manifest on the page. The goal was always to make the whole more meaningful than simply the sum of its parts.

Build me a city.

5.
OWN THE PENALTY

In baseball, the pitcher can throw as many as four un-hittable balls before the batter automatically advances to first base. Each of these four un-hittable balls is considered an error in the pitchers aim, experience, judgement, or ability. That error is a benefit to the batting team. In kubb, the Inkastare is the pitcher and has only two chances to land each kubb inbounds—just one rethrow per kubb. If, after being rethrown a kubb cannot be raised at least 50% in-bounds, it is now a penalty kubb. This penalty kubb can be placed, by the opposing team, anywhere on the opposing team's side of the pitch. Anywhere, save for a single restriction: the kubb must be at least one baton length away from the king or a marking pin. This penalty kubb placement is the only purely defensive move in all of kubb.

While there are a number of strategic advantages to landing

kubbs in the corner or on the center line, there's no rule requiring them to land there. The only requirement is to land them inbounds. There's a full 20 square meters to safely land kubbs within. Missing that huge target, and missing it again, signals the Inkstare's current ambitions are beyond their current abilities.

In the opening round robin of the 2012 US National Kubb Championship, where the Kubbchucks went nearly two matches without hitting a baseline kubb, one of those games was with the formidable Minneapolis-based team of Eric Goplin, Cole Vryens, and Anders Thorstensen—Tad Kubbler. Tad Kubbler opened by toppling a single baseline kubb. The Kubbchucks cold streak mixed poorly with my want to play competitively against a team I'd played dozens of times in the non-competitive setting at Painter Park friendlies. My nervous anxiety overpowered my nascent inkasting ability. I landed this single kubb out of bounds, unquestionably short of the centerline. When I re-threw it, I watched as it landed in just past the centerline—then bounce out the right side of the pitch. Now, I'm also stunned, baffled, disappointed, and embarrassed.

Without a word, Eric Goplin picked up the now penalty kubb and he huddled with the rest of Tad Kubbler to discuss the most strategic placement for it. Minutes later, when they emerged from the huddle, the penalty kubb was placed directly on the baseline. Directly between the two right most baseline kubbs.

Tad Kubbler had watched our last game. They knew we couldn't hit anything at 8 meters.

Jamie, Jim, and I each threw two batons at that penalty kubb. All six batons missed. Tad Kubbler picked up the six batons and expertly toppled their remaining four baseline kubbs followed by the king.

Game over.

The second game of the match went only slightly better. Though we lost the match, our 8-meter cold streak finally broke. Yet, the sting of that first game stayed with us. Jamie and I went back to our team tent and, to exorcise the game from our spirits, we documented the game on the very first version of the Planet Kubb Scoresheet. I'm certain it was the first US National Kubb Championship tournament game ever documented on a scoresheet. I'm also certain it was the worst Championship game ever played.

Tad Kubbler's penalty kubb placement that game was perfect. It showed they knew where our weaknesses were (8 m) and used that knowledge to ensure the penalty kubb ate up at least one baton. It did. It ate all six!

Being able to re-throw a kubb gives the Inksastare the opportunity to correct, to reassess. When the Inkastare is throwing well, the re-throw will have considerably better placement than the first time it was thrown. If the Inksastare doesn't approach the rethrow by checking themselves and checking the state of the pitch—the re-throw will likely land short, or bounce out, or otherwise become a penalty kubb. In the case of the Tad Kubbler game, I didn't make any adjustment for the re-throw. I mindlessly repeated what I just did just a moment ago—except I expected a different outcome. I got the same outcome, with a significantly worse consequence.

Some teams do place the penalty kubb exactly one baton length behind the king. This strategy assumes nerves will cause a baton to hit the king prematurely. This never happens. One baton length behind the king is well within even novice players' short game accuracy. For a right-handed or left-handed player standing in the corner of the pitch a baton-length distance is wide enough to prevent the assumed illegal king hit. Placing the penalty kubb exactly one baton length from the King shows little faith in the opponent's ability, and a preference for the letter of the rulebook over the spirit of the game. Asking for a baton from the throwing team to precisely measure out the distance from the king, while not outside the rules, is the only unsportsmanlike behavior I regularly see on the pitch.

If I'm not sure where a team's weaknesses are, I'll place the penalty kubb around the 6-meter line, on the opposite side of the pitch from the rest of the field kubbs. I may even put it right on the sideline at the 6-meter mark. This placement ensures at least one baton will be spent on the penalty kubb and the chances of a lucky field-to-base kubb bounce are low. If it remains standing—it's a two meter throwing advantage for my team.

#

Back in 2011, before I was even introduced to kubb, before my third child, Augustus, was even a year old, I took on a couple of client projects I shouldn't have. I committed to these atop an already booked schedule and the fatigue of having a newborn in the house. Both of these new client projects were smaller and well outside the definition of my ideal project, but they were for people I thought would be fun to work with. I even had an employee to help out. I thought they'd be challenging-but-do-able projects for people that I wanted to impress and small enough for my employee to be very hands on. Yes, it sounds like an enjoyable way to spend the summer. And yes, bringing in a few extra dollars does prove to my brittle ego that I can provide for my growing family.

Unfortunately, once the projects got underway, they both quickly fell apart. By day two on both, I was kicking myself for agreeing to them. The deadlines were tighter, the expectations higher, and the attitudes were far more dictatorial and far less collaborative than I had anticipated.

All of this made the quoted fees wholly insufficient.

In a heated phone conversation with one of the clients discussing the disconnect in expectations, I confessed I shouldn't have taken on their project in the first place. They were stunned—but we continued on. That weekend, the other project kept me behind a laptop on a beautiful summer day, with the phone's ringer purposefully off, while the rest of the family was swimming in the river. Why was I behind the laptop frazzled and frustrated and not my employee?

It wasn't their fault. They didn't agree to these bad projects. I did. It was my responsibility to divest myself of them as quickly as possible with as minimal collateral damage as possible. That included their sanity and their weekend. As much as I didn't want to do the work either, these were not the kind of hands-on experiences I wanted my employee to have. I just needed to get these projects to a point where I could walk away with a clear conscious.

In the end, both projects did launch when expected. I never did meet my clients' expectations. They never paid my invoices. I'll never work with those people or organizations again. Then again, I never should have in the first place. I was fatigued and playing outside my abilities. These two projects were penalty kubbs.

It took me six months to fire the last of my three employees. I knew after the first month I shouldn't have hired them. Every month, they'd ease my workload just enough for me to be thankful for their involvement, but not substantially enough for me to move my business in the direction I needed it to go. Subconsciously, I was using their involvement as an excuse for me not having the business I wanted.

The truth was: I had made a poor hiring decision (throw 1)

and was an even worse boss (re-throw). My penalty—firing them. There was no other way to progress. No other way to create the business I needed. None of this was the employees' fault. It was all mine—and I needed to take ownership.

#

That penalty kubb isn't the opposing teams fault. They're not to blame. They didn't cause it. Only the Inkastare was active on the pitch at the time. The Inkastare caused it.

Will the opposing team benefit from it? Maybe. They hope so. They might win the game off it. Especially if the Inkastare doesn't take ownership and topple it when it's their turn with the baton.

When the Kubbchucks first started playing, I'd feel badly about my poor inkasting and insist on throwing the first two batons to "clean up the mess." I wouldn't hit anything. I shouldn't have even thrown the batons. The result would have been the same. Except we wouldn't be down one-third of our batons. While throwing kubbs and throwing batons are both throwing wood, they're two very different motions and intentions. Switching immediately from one to another is awkward. Not unlike the bike-run transition in a triathlon. While the motions aren't new or unusual, they are just different enough to initially result in sub-optimal performance. Unfortunately, in kubb "initially" may be just one baton throw.

In practice, to minimize penalty kubbs from stalling my tournament games, I'll inkast deep towards the baseline, or 8 meters on the sideline, even closer to the king than one baton width, or other bizarre locations throughout the pitch. Intentionally landing kubbs in unexpected places removes the shock of having a penalty kubb placed there by someone else. Toppling them with a single baton, also increases my confidence of toppling any kubb anywhere on the pitch.

In tournament play, I step back after throwing in kubbs and let my teammates throw the first few batons (the woodpile is for them anyway). Even that moment of flipping batons behind the line helps me reset mentally and physically. Plus, it gives me plenty of time to focus on the penalty kubb on the other side of the pitch.

That one's mine—I own it.

REBUILDING BLOCKS

6.
MAKE GOOD FENCES

Kubb is a game of equal and opposite forces. The Inkastare's goal is to cluster the field kubbs tightly together as to minimize the number of batons required to topple them. When all the field kubbs have been thrown in, the opposing team's goal is to raise the field kubbs—as far apart as possible, requiring as many batons as possible. The kubbs must be tipped up as if on a hinge connecting them to the ground.

The opposing team only has but a single question to answer with each kubb: raise it on this end or on the other?

The exact same blocks of wood, two opposing goals, one small decision. With a single field kubb, or a bunch of field kubbs all over the pitch, there isn't frequently much discussion among the kubb raisers because spreading this small number of kubbs apart is trivial. However, when an experienced Inkastare stacks a woodpile of 10 kubbs behind the center pin, the entire opposing team may be crouched over the field kubbs to discuss the most defensive raising strategy.

What started as a seemingly simple question has bloomed into a universe of complexity.

From a defensive perspective, the goal is to raise field kubbs in such a way that it increases misses. The more batons eaten up by field kubbs the lower the chance a baseline kubb will be toppled. Everything else is strategy, technique, and mental game.

No matter how the field kubbs are raised, it won't stop the throwing team from progressing to the baseline—it will likely just slow them down. Tipping a field kubb up one direction or another relative to the other field kubbs, relative to whether the throwers are right- or left-handed, and relative to the location of baseline kubbs can all slow down the throwing team more—or less. The formation of field kubbs can create illusions of both ease and complexity. These illusions can trip up experienced players, causing them to throw batons at a chance for a multiple kubb toppling when picking off a single would be more pragmatic.

From a defensive perspective, the ideal field kubb formation is a straight line parallel to the center line—with each kubb more than a baton-length away from the others. This creates a horizontal fence minimizing multiples and fortunate bounces while ensuring one baton per kubb minimum. With seven field kubbs, this formation mathematically guarantees at least one field kubb remains standing, leaving an advantage line. From a defensive perspective, success is that field kubb left standing at the end of six batons. While in actual gameplay it is rare kubbs can be raised exactly in this kind of fence formation—it does provide an easy mental image for novice defenders to remember.

In addition to a fence, there are a handful of surprisingly effective formations I've witnessed in tournament play:

The Goal Post
Raising two field kubbs near each other so they approximate the uprights of an American Football goal post. This formation is tempting and deceptive. It looks like an easy double, if only the baton thrower can get just the right angle. Statistically, though, the first baton thrown will slide in between the two kubbs. As will the next one (especially if the same person is throwing). It's almost if our brains are required to send the baton into the space between the two kubbs. The throwing team can quickly lose four batons chasing the double. I've lost track of how many batons I've seen slide through the goal post—in both tournament and backyard play. I've never seen that double.

Stonehenge
With a large number of field kubbs clustered tightly together, it may be possible to raise them as a ring around one or two center kubbs. This outer ring of field kubbs will protect the inner field kubbs like a city wall. It's a counterintuitive formation to be sure. Those center kubbs look like an easy multiple—once the outer wall is toppled.

Jamie raised this formation in the Kubbchucks vs Kubb Snipers match at the 2012 Dallas Octoberfest tournament. Three batons were lost while blasting through the outer wall. Two more were required for the inner kubbs.

Clustering
Sometimes the most defensive kubb formations are the counterintuitive ones. Two field kubbs in this cluster, three in that cluster, two in another. While the likelihood of multiples are greater for any individual cluster, the clusters themselves

can be far enough apart to ensure a minimum of a single baton each.

The Opposite Line

Imagine the Inkastare lands all the field kubbs in a diagonal line starting at the center pin and progressively moving toward the back middle of the pitch. Depending which side of the pitch this formation is on, it's going to be very difficult line for a right-handed baton thrower or a left-handed thrower because our arms' natural throwing curves the other direction. For a team of all right-handers a formation on pitch left to the back center will be very challenging to topple multiples, where as that same line with a team of all left-handers could be quickly toppled.

#

When raising kubbs, it's tempting to focus just on the lines straight back to the throwing team's base line, this often leaves clear and obvious lines from less obvious angles. Baton throwers can and should use the entire baseline. The kubb raisers should take a moment before committing to raising any kubbs to understand the state of the entire pitch; find the lines from the woodpile to the remaining baseline kubbs, find the lines from the throwing line to the woodpile. Now, develop a vision for the field kubb formation, and know which direction the kubb is to be raised before you touch it.

In your own team, start to develop a language for describing your most defensive formations in a strategic way. It doesn't matter if your shared vocabulary builds off the ones above, just that your team has one. This communication will make your time on the pitch as valuable as possible—which will inherently improve your game.

#

For a long time I found it difficult to set limits on making commitments. I didn't want to miss any opportunities. I wanted to be helpful, liked, and wanted. I'd fulfill low value requests from my clients, I'd get breakfast for the kids immediately when they awoke, I'd accept garbage from my wife when she was standing closer to the garbage can. I jumped at the world's every whim. I wouldn't push back on client requests out of fear of losing them. The only thing I feared more than receiving another tedious request was not receiving another tedious request. I was angry, tired, and filled with resentment and conflict.

Slowly, I started putting up fences.

I deactivated all my Twitter and Facebook accounts. I unsubscribed from every email newsletter that arrived. I turned the spam filter on all my email accounts to "aggressive." I put my phones ringer on silent and kept it there.

If it was before 7 a.m., I would tell the kids that it's not breakfast time, and to go read a book or back to bed.

Though I'd read email messages immediately, I'd wait four hours, six hours, or even a full day before replying thoughtfully and comprehensively as I could to ensure another request didn't arise from it.

I refused to take other people's garbage.

I started going to bed before 11 p.m..

I blocked off two hours every Monday morning to have coffee with my friend, Patrick Rhone. This standing commitment started my week off reviewing my longer term goals rather than a less meaningful client project. For much the same reason, I also blocked off two hours every Friday afternoon to reflect on my business and mentally close out the week.

These days, I still turn the radio off far more than I turn it on, I click "unsubscribe" more frequently than "subscribe", and close the browser window more likely than I'll scroll or click a link. My phone's ringer is silent more often than it's not.

In short, I've built good fences to slow the world down. Good fences. Not impermeable walls with an alligator-filled moat. Just a permeable low-maintenance barrier keeping minor distractions out while allowing in the most important, meaningful, and interesting activities. I can continually adjust the fence's permeability to allow more or less of the world in. Over the past few years this has worked so well I've come to believe the world prefers fences.

Fences clearly define limits and expectations of how to engage. Counterintuitively, it simplifies things for everyone on each side of the fence.

There's a delightful story published in the USA Today on how filmmaker Theodore Melfi cast Bill Murray in Melfi's movie, 'St. Vincent' (*http://www.usatoday.com/story/life/movies/2014/09/05/casting-bill-murray-st-vincent-toronto-film-festival/15148287/*). Melfi called Bill Murray's 1-800 number and left a message. A fairly uninteresting interaction until you consider this lone 1-800 number is how everyone— including Murray's lawyer—contacts Bill. Bill then returns the messages at his convenience. This is such a welcome contrast to business cards listing office phone number, mobile phone number, fax number, email, and multiple Twitter handles.

#

When we moved from Chicago to Minneapolis I started my own company and declared the spare room my office. This

54

continued for two years before any of the kids were born. Those two years gave my wife and me plenty of time to get used to the delicate balance of availability and isolation a home office requires and affords both of us. Early on we agreed that my Work Day starts between 8:30 and 9 a.m. and concludes between 4:30 and 5 p.m.. Again—permeable fences. Some days I may have a client meeting with one of the coasts that shifts outside of those bounds. One of the kids may have a school function or a doctor's appointment that blocks off a couple hours within my normal work day. In both cases, the kids know that when I'm in my office with the door closed—I'm at work and shouldn't be disturbed. The plus side of this is, when I'm not in my office—I'm available.

This availability has led to impromptu lunches of olives, brie, and baguette in the summer sunshine with my oldest daughter. It's led to impromptu lunches at a nearby restaurant with Jen on a random Tuesday afternoon. It's allowed Jen to leave the house, kid-free, during afternoon nap time. It's led to me appreciating and experiencing my young family in ways I wouldn't be able to otherwise. There are downsides. Bathing an infant after a massive diaper blowout while preventing a toddler from making a bigger mess requires two people. It doesn't matter if one of them is about to dial into a client teleconference. Neighborhood kids unaccustomed to parents working from home sometimes stare at me from outside my office as if I'm a zoo exhibit.

Either side of 9 a.m. and 5 p.m. my family becomes the priority—and my professional concerns move to second fiddle. The time between 5 p.m. and 7 p.m. is as an impermeable wall as I have—family dinner time. Within those 90 minutes, the baby needs her dinner, dinner needs to be made and served to the rest of the family, the dining room and living room need to be picked up, and I need to hear the kids share their 'favorite things' of the day. It's a rare professional opportunity that can encroach past 5:30 p.m.. Even within a 9-5 schedule where work is the priority, I have fences. It took me years to admit that my productivity drops considerably after 90 minutes, after five hours, and after 30 hours of concerted effort in a week. Since I've re-committed to owning my own company my intention each week is to average 20 hours of client work, 10 hours of working on my business, and 10 hours of Whatever the Hell I Want—It's My Company! This last category includes visiting the Claes Oldenburg retrospective at the Walker Art Center, brewing beer in the garage, writing this book, shopping without the kids, or playing kubb. All of which, counterintuitively, make me more focused, more present, and more engaged back at my desk.

#

On the pitch, assume the throwing team's Inkastare is talented, fresh, and comfortable. Assume you'll be baffled by how to raise them—let alone form a fence. But you'll find a way and when you step behind your baseline to turn and watch the toppling, you'll get to see a glimpse of disappointment in the eyes of the throwing team. That glimpse tells you that, somehow, you raised the kubbs further apart than they thought possible, that the formation you created was not one they were prepared to topple. This look lasts only a microsecond before the first baton is thrown and proves the most significant fence was raised—the one of doubt in the baton thrower's mind.

7.
CLEAR THE FIELD

A monk told Joshua, "I have just entered the
monastery. Please teach me."

Joshua asked, "Have you eaten your rice porridge?"

The monk replied, "I have eaten."

Joshua said, "Then you had better wash your bowl."

At that moment the monk was enlightened.

(http://www.sacred-texts.com/bud/glg/glg07.htm)

If there are field kubbs, there are only field kubbs. No

baseline kubbs. No king. Only field kubbs.

There is but one outcome for the field kubbs - toppled. All of them. Every turn. Baseline kubbs cannot be toppled until all the field kubbs are gone. The first and only job is to clear the field kubbs. Clearing the field kubbs and not getting a baseline is OK. Not clearing the field and leaving a field kubb standing is not OK. Your opponent can throw their batons from the standing field kubb, wherever it is on the pitch, and dramatically increases their chances of winning the game. Clearing the field kubbs keeps them behind the baseline.

Even six field kubbs is just one kubb per baton. One-for-one. Completely do-able. Yet, the statistics from the 147 games in the Planet Kubb game database
(http://wiki.planetkubb.com/wiki/Game:Main_Page)
indicate this is where even competitive teams leave a field kubb standing. Whether due to a poor inkast, or a tempting double missed more than twice, one kubb frequently remains when six are in the field. Statistics also predict that not toppling the sixth kubb will result in an immediate loss 50% of the time. Even though the number of kubbs increases with each turn, there are only ever six batons. Consistently topple just one field kubb per baton, you'll last longer than many teams. Even in tournament play.

Those field kubbs are all the open loops in your life. They're the emails piling up your inbox. They're the sink of dirty dishes, the stack of drying dishes on the counter, the annoying squeak in your car, the unresolved disagreement with your wife, the unfinished home improvement project. They're your unwashed bowl. I have these things in my life, just as you do. Each of these things uses up our mental energy with their unfinished-ness. Our mind is continually using energy figuring out how to resolve them. This mental energy is the same mental energy you need to make meaningful and significant progress elsewhere in your life.

Yet it's being spent on pondering a sink of dirty dishes.

You need a structure for continually and reliably resolving these issues and releasing that mental energy. There are many. David Allen's *"Getting Things Done"*, Stephen Covey's *"The Seven Habits of Highly Effective People"*, Jim Benson's *"Personal Kanban"*, are a few I've tried. They all have their philosophy, their specialized tools, approaches, and mindset. I found too many of them simply replaced the mental energy of storage with the mental energy of managing lists. After many years of assuming the opposite, I found re-ordering my To Do Lists does not actually complete the work itself. I have built a trusted and resilient four-prong system that works surprisingly well for me; a consistent and reliable daily routine, immediately scheduling everything on my trusted calendar, making fewer—albeit larger—commitments, and giving everything a home.

#

Offensively, the best possible outcome of leaving a field kubb standing is having to topple it once more. You don't lose, you get another turn, but you do start off further behind. Just as leaving a mess for Future You to clean up—when Current You is fully capable—starts you off further away from your goals and with more obligations.

Having the dishwasher full of clean dishes after breakfast is confusing and annoying. The kids will happily put their dirty breakfast dishes in the dishwasher. But this helpful thing quickly turns unhelpful if the dishwasher is filled with clean dishes. Not how I want to start my day. So, every night before bed, I empty the dishwasher (as soon as the kids bedtime is beyond when the dishwasher completes, it will be their job). The evening routine that unloading the dishwasher is part of—that's on my daily calendar. Every night 9:30 p.m.. This routine means I'm not greeted with yesterday's mess the next morning. It took decades before my view of 'cleaning' shifted from one of drudgery, obligation, and annoyance to preparation for tomorrow's success.

As of this writing, my email inbox has been at zero for more than ten months. Every day before I leave the office, I ensure it's empty. Anything I can't answer immediately is scheduled for the next day. Everything else is ruthlessly deleted.

For too long, I'd be late to my commitments because I needed to spend five minutes or more searching for my car keys. Then I bought the Levenger Bomber Messenger bag. It's got a snap for my keys. I know exactly where my keys are right now, they're hanging inside my bag. Similarly, white labels from my well-used labeler can be found on all manila folders, all storage bins, cabinet drawers, and many of the bookshelves in my house. Not only does it help me find stuff when I need it, these labels are clear reminders of where stuff goes when I'm done with it.

The Kubbchucks have always struggled at closing games. Very often we'd have one stranded base kubb and seven field kubbs in play. We could get stuck in a rut with five, six, seven field kubbs. Each turn we'd require all six batons to clear the field kubbs. We'd make no progress on the baseline kubbs, nor would we leave an advantage line. That's how you hang on in a kubb game—by sending all the field kubbs to the other side of the pitch. It's just how you hang on—it's not how you win. Hanging on gives you one more shot at not losing. Winning comes when clearing the field stops being a fight and starts being a routine and a rhythm. Winning comes when clearing the field stops taking mental energy and exceptional effort and starts being a rhythm and routine. When it flows.

As Jamie and I were reviewing the final matches of the 2014 US National Kubb Championship we noticed the average number of batons the winning teams were requiring to clear the field kubbs—2.5. Two-and-a-half batons, on average, to clear 1-10 field kubbs out of six batons. That leaves three batons, two for any remaining base kubbs and one for the king. That's winning. But only after the field is clear.

REBUILDING BLOCKS

8.
LONG GAME WINS

Kubb is actually two games in one; a long game and a short game. The long game is the 8 meter tosses to the baseline kubbs on the other side of the pitch. The short game is blasting at the field kubbs wherever they stand. The long game is the same for everyone, the same five baseline kubbs equally spaced at the same 8 meter distance. Same for me, same for you. The short game, changes on every turn and with every baton. The short game is dependent on how well the Inkastare groups the field kubbs and how many multiples the First Blaster topples.

The short game is dramatic, intense, and high pressure.

Both games require different approaches and different throws. My goal with each throw between 4 meter and 8 meter is to vertically rotate the baton in the air 180°—so the back end rotates towards the ground before rotating up and hitting the bottom half of the target kubb. When I'm throwing 4 meters or less—for example a short game with any advantage line—I'll sometimes use a similar throw. Other times, I'll release the baton so it strikes the kubb vertically and the bottom of the baton hits the top of the nearest field kubb.

Sometimes, we fixate on the drama and intensity of the short game. I'll admit I've spent significantly more time working on my inkasting and short game than I have on my 8 meter shots. Part of my focus on the short game has to do with improving my strategy and controlling the multitude of variables in the short game. There is also the delight in knocking over three, four, or five field kubbs with a single baton at close range.

But here's the thing.

The primary goal in kubb is to topple the five baseline kubbs. All field kubbs must be toppled before toppling baseline kubbs. Knocking over the king with baseline kubbs standing is forfeiting—not winning. The way to the baseline kubbs is through the field kubbs. Do so as efficiently as possible. Ideally no more than one baton—no matter how many field kubbs.

The short game can also be very deceptive. A tight cluster of field kubbs can appear to be a straight-forward double, triple, or quad. Then reality strikes. The baton cartwheels over all the kubbs, or only the middle one topples, or the baton shoots right between all of them—like a football through the field goal uprights. I've see so many variations of these kinds of misses in backyard play and in tournament play, in scored games in the Planet Kubb Game database. No matter how attractive a grouping of field kubbs looks, a single baton will on average topple only two. Even at the highest level of play. Getting distracted by the drama of the short game can actually be detrimental to your goal of winning.

You can't win on the short game. You can only win on the long game.

Just like life.

Laundry, groceries, housekeeping, commutes, errands, entertainment, the constant maintenance of banality—all short game. Yes, they can bring a lot of joy and drama to our lives. Yes, not taking care of them appropriately and effectively makes achieving our intended goals more tenuous—that's the definition of short game.

The long game: satisfying relationships with family and friends, meaningful work, fulfilling avocations—these things take decades to achieve. These things require persistence, discretionary time, and focused time free of short game.

#

For the first 13 years of my career, I thought I could win on the short game: the next client, the next opportunity. I entered the professional world on the front end of the dot com boom just as CD-ROMs were busting. I had skills in both. I never spent more than nine months at any employer. Either they went out of business or I found a better offer. Sometimes both happened in the same week. I felt like I was riding an ever increasing wave of success.

Then the bottom fell out.

Airplanes were flown into the World Trade Center a week before I was to take a new job at an agency specializing in online travel. I was still hired. Six months later all online travel projects dried up. Thankfully, a few months later, they came back and I was asked to help out with one of the more formidable web re-platforming projects I've ever worked on. This project set the foundation for me going out on my own. However, once on my own, I continued my focus on the next thing, and the next thing after that. I didn't realize that each successive "next" was actually smaller and more frivolous than the previous, quickly replaced by another, smaller more frivolous "next" tomorrow. I felt like I was on a steadily increasing treadmill I didn't control. Frantic, burnt out, and exhausted, I stepped off the treadmill and onto the kubb pitch.

Initially, my long term goals were: play kubb every day and topple one kubb at 8 meters with six batons.

Once I broke the habit of replacing every waking moment in my calendar with client work, I had this nagging sense that I actually didn't know what I should be doing. After neglecting myself for so long, I didn't even know what my most important work was any more. I needed to find an answer.

I started by writing down every slightly interesting idea that came to mind. Soon I filled a letter-size paper with scores of potential Cool Project Ideas. Yet, none of them felt meaningful enough to even start. So, I headed to the self-help section of the library. After dozens of books and hundreds of recommended exercises. The answer came from my deathbed.

In Gay Hendricks's book, *"Five Wishes"*, he asks you to imagine yourself with just moments to live- just enough breaths remaining to articulate why your life was unsuccessful. The clarity, honesty, and urgency of the answers from this exercise are echoed in *"The Tools"* by Phil Stutter and Barry Michele.

I grabbed another sheet of paper and imagined my death. Dying Me began to speak. At the top of the crisp, clean, white sheet of paper I wrote: "I never felt liberated."

What? Where did this come from? What do I need to feel liberated from? I grab another sheet of paper, continue to transcribe. Answers fill the page, most of them echoing my current burnout, depression, and anxiety. But one stood out against all these others: "I never felt liberated from the feelings of abandonment caused by my parents divorcing."

A few months later, after our fourth child, Penelope, was born, I enlisted M. Gary Neumann's *"The Long Way Home"* plan to help me resolve the twenty-year old-trauma of my parents divorcing. The program was gut-wrenchingly difficult. Each journalling session left me more emotionally drained than I already was. Throughout it, I had a far shorter fuse and was far more difficult to be around than I expected. Today, as I approach a year from concluding the program, those feelings of abandonment no longer haunt me. Nor do I sense those dark leviathans lurking just below my conscience. I've never felt more confident as a husband, as a father, or in my own skin.

All told, the initial "unsuccessful life" writing exercise generated only handful of projects—yet all of them are substantially meaningful to me. None of them were about creating a hot iPhone app, nor about leading a dot com through a hockey stick growth curve, or running for President. Only one of them was on the original Cool Project Ideas list. All of the projects were about better appreciating my family's heritage, making art that can persist for decades, inspiring others to be independent, and writing a shelf of books. All of them are long game. These projects will take me years or decades to achieve. All along the way, I'll still need to buy groceries, pay the mortgage, vacuum the stairs, and empty the dishwasher. Yet, even having defined this small handful of life projects has had a surprising outcome. The short game no longer feels burdensome—it just is. Today's hot, new thing becomes easy to miss. My horizon has shifted to determining what progress I can make on these Successful Life Projects over the next year, next five years, and next decade.

Breaking down the 10,000 hours of deliberate practices Malcolm Gladwell hypothesizes is required to achieve any level of expertise: 10,000 hours = 6 hours per day * 365 days per year * 4.6 years. Nearly five years of deliberate practice and incremental progress. The intensity and persistency means the resulting outcome isn't something you can purchase in a single transaction, rather it's something that will continue to be meaningful while capturing your imagination, continuously. Most importantly—it's something that will be a meaningful asset on the other side of those 10,000 hours.

For those of you with children, you're well aware of the astounding differences a year can make in a child. Babies walk. Toddlers crack jokes. School-age kids actually help around the house. Progress toward your goals is the same. On a daily basis it's difficult to see small incremental progress, yet in aggregate—transformative.

I'm able to trace my van Buren line to what is now Albany, New York more than a hundred years before the United States was declared. Two of my ancestors on another line fought in the Revolutionary War. Two more of my ancestors settled in the city I currently reside—46 years before it was a city. Based on my lineage, I can plan on another four decades of life—with even modest advances in quality of life technologies—six decades is more likely. Yet, I could be gone tomorrow due to forces beyond my control. There is meaningful, substantial work that only I can do. Just as there is meaningful, substantial work that only you can do. The odds are we can post-pone this work until tomorrow. By no means is my longevity guaranteed. Once I'm gone, the chances that my Successful Life projects are completed falls to zero.

#

As the Kubbchucks Inkastare I'm responsible for tossing the field kubbs in a tight cluster to be efficiently toppled by the rest of the team. I'm responsible for minimizing the burden of my team's short game.

As I write this, my preference is to cluster the kubbs just in front of the centerline, so when tipped up they're just 50% in-bounds. The shortest game possible. Some Inkastares like to cluster tight into the corner of the mid-line and the sideline. The center pins sometimes spook the Kubbchucks, so I aim a little more inside the center pin than others may prefer. My second preference is inkast deep. Real deep. To me, the perfect inkast is right in front of a base kubb. So close that when the field kubb topples a baseline kubb topples with it. This placement has a wonderful competitive advantage—it clears the field kubbs while minimizing any potential advantage line to your opponent. Assuming you've got a good long game.

Inkasting deep blurs the lines between short game and long game. Being able to land and hit field kubbs anywhere on the pitch opens up strategies and approaches that don't exist when the short and long games are distinct from one another. For example, imagine your opponent opens the game by toppling all five baseline kubbs. The most competitive response is to inkast all five field kubbs in front of a base kubb, topple the five field kubbs and a baseline kubb with the first baton. Then topple the remaining four baseline kubbs with one baton a piece. Leaving the sixth baton for the king. An aggressive response to be sure. One that's all about a good long game. No, I've never seen a team respond this way in tournament play.

Off the pitch, I've reduced the amount of energy, decision-making, and overall cognitive load required for life's short game in three ways; the first is to immediately schedule tasks on my calendar when I think of them, put everything in its home, and have a deliberate morning routine. My morning routine is currently flossing, shaving, cleaning my glasses, and 15 other banal tasks. It didn't start that way. It started with flossing my teeth after showering and marking on the wall calendar that I did it. Two things. If I forgot, I'd run up to the bathroom as soon as I remembered. Once the showering and flossing habit was established I added additional task—clean my glasses. Same process, cross it off on the calendar when completed, do it immediately if I realized I hadn't yet. This rhythm and routine provide a structure to my day. This structure helps me make fewer small decisions, so I can focus on the bigger ones. I don't need to decide what to have for breakfast, or when I should floss, or when I should clean my glasses. Those decisions have been made. I just need to execute. Less energy on short game means more energy for the long game.

Over the next 30 days I have a goal to hit five baseline kubbs sequentially and consistently. Sure, once I have it down, I'd only be able to perform it in singles tournaments and backyard play. This goal is more about developing the rhythm, comfort and control to consistently hit 8m. A skill will serve me in every tournament I compete in, and every game I play. It may even provide me with insights on improving my short game. Again, it's as much about the result as it is about the long term journey.

Kubb can be played competitively for as long as you can accurately throw a baton 8 meters. Even if I'm not able to consistently hit 5-for-5 this summer, I could have another 60 summers in front of me to achieve it. To me, having a game I could play with not only my children, but my grandchildren, and maybe even great-grandchildren, that's winning at the long game.

9.
NOBODY'S PERFECT

Kubb isn't particular about the surface its played on. Man-made surfaces like asphalt, concrete, artificial turf are acceptable, they're also so rigid and impermeable as to create unpredictable bounces and wear down the corners of the kubbs more quickly. But if that's what's available—that's what's available. The lush green grass and rich top soil at the suburban soccer park, your backyard, even the hard, clover-covered parks in Uptown Minneapolis are preferred because they give—even a little. The kubbs should stick when thrown in and the batons should slide just a little bit. This is as much about control and consistency as it is about not having to continually chase down game pieces. The pitch surface should be comfortable to bare feet on a warm summer day. That's how I prefer to play in tournaments—barefoot. It provides me with a greater understanding of the playing surface and how the wood will perform. Playing barefoot is also a reminder of kubb's simplicity, honesty, and directness. Shoes are an awkward reminder of the interfaces required to interact with the real world.

If you've played kubb before you've likely noticed that the opening team has six batons to knock over six targets (five baseline kubbs and a king). Successfully doing so is the definition of the Perfect Game. I've only see this happen in practice sessions and backyard play—never in the three years of competitive tournament play I've experienced. Yet, it is a potentiality within the structure of the game, six batons—six targets. I find it odd that throughout the history of the game (either 30 years or 300 years) that the number of batons hasn't been reduced to five or the number of baseline kubbs raised to six. Nothing structurally has changed the possibility of a Perfect Game. It's almost as if this potentiality exists to give high-level players something to continuously debate.

The legality of the Perfect Game is one of the two defining differences between the World Championship rules and the US National Kubb Championship rules. In the US, the Perfect Game is not permitted as it's unsportsmanlike to win against an opponent who hasn't yet thrown a single baton. Toppling all six targets on an opening turn doesn't allow the opposing team to show what they're made of. From this perspective, the Perfect Game definitely goes against the sports' unofficial motto of "uniting people and creating peace". If you're playing under the US ruleset—and you open the game by toppling five baseline kubbs—you surrender your sixth baton to the other team. Worth noting, there is no restriction against an answering team getting a Perfect Game.

In Europe, where play is under World Championship rules and the Perfect Game is legal, tournament organizers are continually exploring different mechanisms to reduce the chance of a Perfect Game; halving the number of batons the opening team throws (Basil 3 Open) or by having the opening team throw in one of their baseline kubbs immediately (increasing their number of initial targets to seven).

Even still, the Perfect Game is extremely rare even at the highest level of competitive play. Again, I've never seen a team open with five baseline kubbs in three years of scoring the US Championship. After surviving the round of 16, a team is far more likely to miss every baseline kubb out of fatigue and nerves than forfeit the sixth baton. Yet, it is a possibility, a potential, a measure of your ability, and when achieved, a celebration. The strategies currently designed to eliminate the Perfect Game; the etiquette of forfeiting the sixth baton, the complexity of opening with fewer batons, and the baseline kubb surrender—these are nuances to be remembered, enforced, and agreed to. They all replace an admitted flaw in the number of game pieces with a negotiation.

The Perfect Game exists in our everyday lives as well. Or rather, the mythological possibility of it. The Perfect Partner, the Perfect Kids, the Perfect Job, the Perfect Diet, the Perfect Car, the Perfect House, the Perfect School. Structurally, it looks like it's possible to achieve. Structurally, there doesn't seem to be anything keeping us from them. But of course, our nerves frequently get the best of us, our ability isn't as developed as we hoped, or simply we self-sabotage ourselves.

2012 was my first trip to the US National Kubb Championship in Eau Claire, Wisconsin. A client encouraged me to introduce myself to Aaron Ellringer. From watching footage on YouTube of past tournaments, I knew Aaron was one of the top US kubb players. He and his dad won the Championship just two years prior. This year he was playing with his son. His inkasting style was distinctive and consistent, his baton hits were solid. There was a calm, monk-like aura about him on and off the pitch. I introduced myself and referred to our mutual friend. After we shook hands, he bluntly asks,

"It looks like you've got a pretty good life—why do you want kubb to mess it up?"

Yes, from the outside it looked like I had a pretty good life. I was about to pass my decade anniversary of working for myself, I had a loving wife, three kids, a mortgage on a 1950s rambler in the suburbs, and I was able to step away from all of it for the US National Kubb Championship. Pretty good, by no means Perfect. On the inside I was a mess—an anxious, brittle, self-hating, mess. Whether it was about making the next week's payroll, being a supportive husband, a loving father, a valuable vendor, or anything else. On every issue I felt I was punching above my weight. This tournament was one of the first constructively selfish things I had done in years, decades likely. Selfishly, obsessively, for me.

Ironically, relative to Aaron's question, kubb was my rock. Kubb was the foundation I was rebuilding my life upon. Without kubb, rather than meeting new people outside on a beautiful summer day—I'd be cowering behind a computer screen in my basement.

In college, I knew my goal was to work for myself. Yet, at no point did I write down "Be my own boss" or "Work for myself." It seems as inevitable as aging itself. Then, before I turned 30, I was president of a corporate entity, invoicing clients, depositing checks into a corporate account, and paying myself a regular salary, all from the spare bedroom. Unfortunately, I didn't really believe it. It all seemed just so flimsy and abstract. Of course, any day now someone will offer me a position at an actual, corporate entity. Any. Day. Now. Oh, well, the mortgage is still due, I'll keep pursuing consulting engagements.

The day Augustus, my third child was born, I looked into his clear blue eyes and I was met with a, "Are you serious? About working for yourself, I mean. Are you actually serious about making that—work?"

Um.

He was right to ask. One kid didn't significantly impact my lack of work life balance. Two kids are more than twice as challenging—they brought me right up to the line of needing to rethink my life—but I never crossed it. Three kids however. Three kids...

To be perfectly honest—I wasn't serious. I hadn't been serious. For a decade. I was walking backward. Always reacting, never working towards a bigger vision. I needed to decide. Get serious or get a damn job.

"Fine, fine," I replied in a sleep-deprived panic, "OK, I'm serious."

Off I went, fatigued and panicked, meeting with more clients, closing more business, booking more projects, promptly overwhelming my calendar and my still sleep-deprived self.

Despite the many strong recommendations against the idea, I hired employees. Just as I was warned, rather than lightening my workload they amplified its complexity. I now needed to ensure they were doing that magic combination of work they were good at, work the client asked for, and work I wanted to sell. The work they were good at wasn't valuable enough to cover their costs let alone my managerial overhead. Each month's payroll tax filing gave a price to both my frustration and my procrastination.

Since then, I've fired all my employees and continually revisited the question Augustus asked me the day he was born. It took me a few years, but I finally understand his question. It wasn't really about working for myself—it was about knowing why I was. Beyond "nobody's hired me yet" I had never answered why I wanted to work for myself. Six reasons came to mind immediately:

- To spend time with him, his siblings, and my wife throughout the banality of the day;

- To be in control of my work environment;

- To have low overhead so I can be selective and excited about the clients I engage;

- To provide my clients a value-rich, intimate, and unique engagement;

- To focus on providing my clients results to their most challenging problems; and

- To continually provide opportunities for my own personal and professional development.

My behavior over the past decade of business did not reflect those six intentions.

#

In the opening round robin of the 2012 US National Kubb Championship, anxiety and self-doubt won me over. The Kubbchucks and I went cold. We couldn't hit a baseline kubb for the better part of two games. Jim, Jamie, and I, three middle-aged family men, with successful careers, completely fell apart in front of a nice father-mother-son team from Elk Mound, Wisconsin. I felt we should be able to beat them easily and we choked. The kid may have been throwing helicopters, but we weren't throwing anything. I was all caught up in the disconnect between how well I expected to play and how poorly I was playing.

I turned away from the pitch. It was as much an attempt to allow the beauty of the open green fields to calm my nerves as it was refusing to witness us fall even further behind. It didn't work. I still assumed I could achieve the Perfect Life. I assumed I could have it all: wife, kids, house, vocation, avocation, ego. I assumed I could have it all so easily without really doing the hard work. But, I was playing under the US ruleset. I needed to forfeit that sixth baton—my ego.

Once I accepted my abilities for what they were—however undeveloped—only then were we able to come together as a team. We were able to eke out of the round robin with just enough wins to compete for the last Championship bracket slot. After two long games against The Engineers the Kubbchucks prevailed.

In kubb, the defense is so minimal as to be nonexistent. Your opponent's core defensive move is to decide which side to raise field kubbs on. While this can present surprising results —no possibility is significantly unplayable. This means you're always playing kubb against yourself, against your own nerves. It's the worst version of you that throws every baton. Whether you hit a kubb or miss a kubb—it was you and you alone that did that. The most raw, most naked, most vulnerable, and most ill-prepared part of you. That's your opponent. Not the team on the other side of the pitch.

It was a beautiful Saturday morning in late June, for the 2014 Minnesota Kubb Open tournament in downtown Minneapolis. Jim and I were playing as the Kubbchucks. We should have played under a different name, or better, just stayed home. Our play was abysmal. My 8 meter throws were closer to 9, my inkasting was all over the pitch, Jim's short game was just a little too. The worst versions of us were on the pitch that day. The only match we won was against a team that didn't show up. At the end of the opening round robin we were sent to the Consolation Bracket. In the Consolation Bracket we were promptly eliminated. There was nothing in our performance that day to be proud of. Only we were to blame. The only saving grace was that Jim and I were communicating. We were discussing game strategy, about who should throw when, about how we should throw. While our performance was weak, we were connecting in a stronger way as teammates. Unfortunately, this stronger communication couldn't save us from teams that could actually hit kubbs.

Artisans of many ancient cultures intentionally placed flaws in their works. Whether Persian rugs, Amish quilts, or Navajo pottery, these flaws are marketed as a humbling reminder that they were human and perfection was limited to the gods. Gods who don't need to get wares to market or have bills to pay. Humans run out of raw material, time, energy, and patience. These restrictions should focus our minds on achieving our largest, most important goals and a few, small flaws are a small price to pay for a conclusion.

Perfectionism at it's core is about a lack of confidence and a fear of being vulnerable. The projects where I needed to control every detail, the ones I needed to be perfect before sharing with anyone, those projects failed the hardest and most spectacularly. In the end, I did not achieve the perfection I was striving for and I solved things nobody else cared about. In fact, most things in our world, outside of sport, are so complex that perfect cannot be anything other than subjective. Which is why perfectionists are so damn busy, they're attempting to create something that not only they deem as flawless but all others that encounter it. All with a very minimal and continually changing definition of Perfect. That's prescription for frustration and defeat. Professionally, once I realized how little can actually be discussed and agreed to within a review meeting—I stopped stressing out about how much more needed to be done ahead of the meeting. I worked toward solving the biggest problems with the information I had, acknowledging the information I lacked, and being open to dramatically unexpected unknown information presenting itself in the client meetings. That meant many things I wanted to improve were left untouched, and that I needed to keep focused on the most hairiest, most difficult, most uncomfortable problems. Sometimes never to my satisfaction, but significant progress within all of the constraints. Perfection doesn't deliver.

The US National Kubb Championship rules don't allow a Perfect Game, not because it's not structurally possible, but because under the current US Championship rules the Perfect Game really isn't. See, World Championship rules require a minimum of six players per team—with no player throwing more than one baton. To achieve a Perfect Game under those conditions each of the six players needs to hit the intended target with their single baton. Everyone 100% accurate. Most definitely, a celebration, an accomplishment. The current US Championship rules require teams with a minimum of three people and no player throwing more than two batons. Three people with 100% accuracy, while difficult, is less than half as difficult to achieve as getting six people with 100% accuracy. You yourself may be so consistent and skilled that you can reliably topple five kubbs at 8 meters all tournament long. Impressive. But, a Perfect Game is not an individual accomplishment—it's a six-person team accomplishment. You'll need five teammates as passionate and focused to work toward your same goal. This means the Perfect Game is an expression of teamwork, camaraderie, support, and salesmanship. These characteristics are unattainable to an individual.

While nobody's perfect, perhaps together we can be.

10.
DEFINE YOUR METRICS

The park's brown grass was still crunchy with frost at the 2012 Oktoberfest tournament in Dallas, Wisconsin—the only six-person tournament in the US This was the second time the Kubbchucks met the Kubb Snipers in tournament play. It was only our third tournament and though we had recovered from the beating we took at the US Championship I knew we still weren't strong enough to beat the Kubb Snipers. Especially with the seven-person team we cobbled together at the last minute. My seven-year old son, more interested in playing on the park's playground equipment, alternated with a guy from Iowa more interested in the Oktoberfest.

I knew a loss was eminent, I just wanted to hold it off as long as possible. If we weren't going to win, I needed a different metric to measure how we were performing against the team ranked #3 in the US and #4 in the world. I knew the Kubb Snipers, even a six-person Kubb Snipers, would convert any advantage line we left to a win immediately. I wanted to at least make them work for the win. My goal for the match was to not leave a single field kubb standing. Even though the Kubb Snipers toppled the king—I was celebrating. We achieved that goal on the first game. We did it. Unfortunately, we were unable to maintain it through the second game, and just as I expected, the first field kubb we left standing was used to quickly topple the remaining baseline kubbs and then the king.

The Kubb Snipers won the match.

Unlike many other endeavors, you don't win on points in kubb. Nor can you wait out the clock. In tournament play, the best two-out-of-three matches are limited to one hour simply to keep the tournament moving forward. The end of the game, however, is clear and straight-forward—the king is toppled. However definitive, it does make measuring your improvement more challenging. Especially for new players not yet strong enough to win against more experienced teams.

This idea of measuring improvement at a more granular level than wins was one of the reasons Jamie Thingelstad and I developed the Planet Kubb Game Notation. We also wanted a way to quickly document, store, and communicate kubb game play. With enough games recorded it's easy to track a team's improvement across games, tournaments, seasons. With even a few games documented, even all losses, you can answer some performance-oriented questions like:

- How much higher is the percentage of our batons that toppled kubbs compared to our last match?

- How much higher is the percentage of field

kubbs we toppled with the first baton from the
same tournament last year?

- How many more penalty kubbs did we throw
  this year verses last year?

- How much better are we now compared to
  then?

Notice none of these questions are about the number of
toppled kings. They're about all the work to get a shot at the
king. These are things you can track while practicing in your
backyard solo or with your teammates.

The Planet Kubb Game Notation represents each significant
action in the game with a single letter—misses, kubb hits,
kubbs inkast, everything—for each baton (or kubb) thrown.

Baton Throws
- miss
B base kubb hit
F field kubb hit
K king hit
= missed king

Kubb Throws
I number of kubbs inkast
R number of kubbs re-thrown
P number of penalty kubbs

From the inkast to the sixth baton, entire games can be
quickly documented. If the game was documented in the
Planet Kubb Scoresheet, two key performance metrics can
be quickly calculated for both sides of the pitch:

First Baton Efficiency:
The total percentage of field kubbs toppled
with the first baton of the turn.

This statistic measures the level of performance of both the Inkastare and the First Blaster, and how quickly a team can clear the field kubbs.

Hit %:
The total percentage of batons that toppled something.

This statistic measures a team's overall accuracy. Anything above 50% will be competitive in most tournaments, even the US Championship. The closer to 60% it is, the more likely you'll win the tournament. An easy metric to keep in mind during backyard play.

About the same time in 2012 as Jamie and I were developing the Planet Kubb Game Notation, there was another group working on a different method of recording kubb play. It was just a few days before the US National Kubb Championship and many of the top US players were meeting in Painter Park in the Uptown neighborhood of Minneapolis for some non-competitive play. Jamie and I were recording some games with an early version of the Planet Kubb Game Notation. On the other side of the park, was the other group doing the same with their own. The biggest difference Jamie and I saw, they were recording every detail.

Which side of the kubb did the baton graze?

How far away did the baton stop?

While interesting, and perhaps useful from a training perspective, Jamie and I felt this level of detail was far too granular to be meaningful in recording high-speed tournament play. While much of the nuance and subtlety documented by the other group's method is lost in the Planet Kubb Game Notation, the metrics indicating game progress are captured.

The only time I step onto the pitch with the goal of winning is at tournaments. Other times—in my backyard, at friendlies —I'm most likely working on some other goal. As of this writing, I'm working on three kubb-related goals:

- **Topping five baseline kubbs in a row.**
  So far I've done it three times. Lots of time gotten three in a row. A few times—four in a row. Lots more times I've missed all five. While only in singles tournament will I even have a chance to attempt 5-for-5 in tournament play, this goal improves my consistency at 8 meters. Consistency there helps me everywhere.

- **Inkast ten kubbs in such a way that each is touching at least one other kubb.**
  I've yet to achieve this. My maximum so far is six. Even then, there's likely one or two kubbs halfway across the pitch from the woodpile. For me, a good inkast is measured by the number of people crouched around the woodpile baffled by how to raise the kubbs. Having the kubbs touch, overlap, and land atop each other increases the complexity in the kubb raising.

- **Inkast ten kubbs right on either the sideline or centerline so they can only be raised in one direction.**
  This leaves no options for raising by the opposing team. My high in backyard practice has been five: three on the sideline and two on the centerline. Both this goal and the kubb touching goal are about controlling the inkast from when the kubb is thrown to when it's raised.

All three of these goals, and others, are included in the goals notebook I review every morning and rebuild every month. In this notebook I write down my progress towards the goals that are most important to me over the next 30 days, next year, next five years, and next decade. For just like kubb— there's no winning on points in life. There is on making significant progress on meaningful metrics.

Just as cars going the same direction on the same highway at the same speed may not have the same destination—you and I may have different measures of success. Even despite our similarities.

A larger house, a fancier office, an ever growing team of employees, record breaking revenues, thousands of miles of business travel each year—these were my monkey brain's success metrics. These were the metrics driving me into my basement, separating me from my family and viewing everyone as a competitor for my piece of the pie.

Once I started to appreciate what I had, who I was, and what I wanted for myself—my success metrics dramatically changed. Today my meaningful metrics are controlling my time, controlling my commitments, and making substantial progress on my Successful Life Projects. Things either fall into those three buckets or they don't. Rather than measuring total revenues, I measure the percentage of revenue I earned from those efforts consistent with my long-term goals. No guilt, no envy, no regret on anything else.

I've found the most reliable method of tracking progress towards meaningful goals to be pen and paper. Electronic gadgets are too unreliable—both in the short term and in the long term. Batteries die, hardware wears out, software flakes out and is no longer supported. Paper persists for decades. Legend has it Jerry Seinfeld honed his comic ability by writing jokes everyday and crossing off the day in the wall calendar when he did. The measurable metric? A long, unbroken streak of Xs.

I still mark on my wall calendar when I've completed everything in my morning routine, when I've zero-ed out my email inbox for the day, when I'm in bed before 10 p.m., when I naturally awake before 5:30 a.m..

I've found it takes me 26 continuous days to install a new daily habit. I first noticed this specific duration with my "Achieve Inbox 0 Daily" Seinfeld calendar. On the 26th consecutive day of Inbox 0, I made the mistake of checking my email outside of the designated time and a message was sitting there that I couldn't immediately do anything with. If I left it marked 'unread' I'd break my 26-day streak, but I can't act on this message right now. What did I do? I quickly scheduled 30 minutes on the next day's calendar to re-read and act on this specific message. I've maintained Inbox 0 ever since.

So many of the goals we've talked about so far are about mastering basic skills, maintaining good habits, having a system in place, having a routine in place, having an answer at the ready, being prepared. In a points-oriented endeavor like baseball or basketball you may be able to get some number on the scoreboard without having the basics down. In kubb, without points, solid foundation skills are a prerequisite for success.

My recommitment to being a successful Corporation of One required me to dramatically change my mindset about work, clients, and the value I provide. I had to shake off a well-ingrained mindset of billing hourly (since I never enjoyed it, it didn't take long), I had to build a new foundation of how to talk about my professional services and who to talk about them with. Along the way, I found people who value my involvement far more than those paying hourly ever did. Namely—me.

The Kubbchucks second year at the U. National Kubb Championship in 2013 we had a modest goal—relax, play well, actually enjoy the tournament. We easily won all our Round Robin matches. We played so well that unlike the previous year, we didn't need a play-in match to land in the Championship bracket, we were already there. Mission accomplished. Sure, we were eliminated from the tournament on our next match—in exactly the same place we were the previous year. But, we didn't work nearly as hard. That's a huge sign of progress.

In 2014 my goal was to advance deeper into the Championship bracket. Ideally, playing the quarterfinals on Sunday morning and tying for fifth place. That goal starts with consistently, reliably hitting baseline kubbs at 8 meters and inkasting field kubbs in a bafflingly tight woodpile. While our play improved somewhat over the past year, everyone else's play improved substantially. We again needed to fight for our spot in the Championship bracket. We were again eliminated from the tournament at that exact same spot.

11.
Get Better

On August 19, 2012, just a few weeks after my exhausting debut at the 2012 US Kubb National Championship, Eric Anderson from USA Kubb interviewed Terry Ekelöf of Sweden's Team Ekeby on his team's 12th World Championship win (http://www.ustream.tv/recorded/24822758). For 90 minutes, Eric and Terry discussed every esoteric aspect of competitive kubb: which angle to consider baton throws illegal, whether it's good sportsmanship to place the penalty kubb behind the king, and when to inkast kubb deep into the pitch.

Terry's advice on all these topics: "Get better."

Is your opponent consistently toppling kubbs with questionable baton throws?

"Get better."

Did you lose a game because the penalty kubb was placed directly behind the king?

"Get better."

Did you lose a game because you left a field kubb at 4 meters?

"Get better."

Terry's advice is as optimistic, pragmatic, timeless, and matter-of-fact as the game of kubb itself.

Unlike other endeavors, the team on the other side of the kubb pitch has very little ability to impact your performance negatively. There are only two defensive moves: determining which side of a kubb to raise and where to place a penalty kubb. In both cases, the Inkastare completely controls the opponent's ability to exercise these moves. Kubb is less like two opposing teams in battle and more like two teams playing against themselves on the same pitch at the same time. In this scenario, there is only one way to ensure a win: Get better.

I had too many obligations, too many responsibilities. I had too much to do. I was a father of three, a husband, with a mortgage, a car payment, five health care premiums, a weekly grocery bill, a gasoline bill, multiple client deadlines, and a suburban lawn to mow. Each day a new obligation was stacked atop the others. Each day the stack of obligations weighed heavier on me than the day before. In my mind, I was pulling a rusty Red Rider wagon overflowing with these obligations up a sandy mountain trail. Alone. All of these things I agreed to. All of these things I accepted. Underneath them all I was brittle, empty, exhausted, and in tears. Underneath them all, I was failing. I knew I needed to do something. I knew that improving my situation was my responsibility—one more responsibility atop the wagon.

I wasn't taking care of myself. I was sick with a mixture of depression, workaholism, and self-hate. I had been sick for so long—decades likely—I didn't even realized things could be different. I just knew I could not be sick any longer.

"Get better."

"I'm not doing so well right now"

"Get better."

These two words became a solid, hopeful foundation for me to step onto. I still didn't know what "better" looked like, just that the first step meant playing more kubb. It meant play kubb whenever I found myself staring at my computer monitor not knowing what to do next. Play kubb when I had a hard decision to make and needed some distance from the problem. When I first started throwing wood in the backyard in the middle of the afternoon, I'd continuously be interrupted. Not by my family. Not by my neighbors. But by my monkey brain ego declaring there was something more important—and work-related—I should be working on.

"No. This is what I'm doing right now. This is the most important thing right now. I'm getting better."

If I could hold the voice at bay while focusing on that base kubb 8 meters away—both would topple. When the weather didn't support me going outside, I substituted the kubb session for mindful meditation. The challenge in quieting this voice is in acknowledging it and not reacting. Nothing it demands is ever the most important use of my time, just another distraction. Once I was able to consistently quiet the monkey brain and all its frantic, petty demands on my time, I could see all the sound and fury masked a deep, underlying unease; I needed to explore it. After neglecting myself for so long, I didn't even know what I wanted anymore. I needed to find out.

All along the journey of rebuilding myself, block by block, kubb was there. Patient, welcoming, honest.

One summer night in 2014, Eric Goplin and I were talking game strategy in Painter Park. He told me, "You lose from the weakest part of your game, once you improve that, you'll lose by the next weakest part of your game."

Bright lights cast shadows. Improvement in one area of our lives reveals a deficiency in another.

Get better.

Appendix I.
How to Play Kubb

First Things First

- Create an 8-meter by 5-meter rectangle.

- Place the king in the middle

- Place five kubbs, equally spaced, on each 5-meter side

- Make two teams

Who Goes First?

- On the count of three—one person from each team

throws a single baton toward the king

- The team with the baton closest to the king —without knocking it over—selects to go first or which side they'd like to start from.

Game On!

- Each team now takes turns throwing each of the six batons at the five baseline kubbs on the other side of the pitch.

- Each kubb knocked over during a turn is thrown into the field—past the king—at the beginning of the next team's turn. These field kubbs are tipped up, as if on a hinge, by the opposing team and must all be knocked down before attacking any remaining baseline kubbs.

- If a field kubb remains standing at the end of a turn, the opposing team may move up to the location of this kubb for their six throws.

For the Win

- The first team to knock over all the field kubbs, all the remaining baseline kubbs, and the king—wins!

Appendix II.
World Kubb Resources

Belgium
kubbspel.be

Canada
kubbcanada.com

Des Moines Kubb
desmoineskubb.com

England
kubbuk.org

Germany
dkubbb.de

Planet Kubb
planetkubb.com

Global Team Rankings and Game Database
wiki.planetkubb.com

Game Notation and Scoresheets
planetkubb.com/score

Sweden
kubbistan.se

www4.idrottonline.se/KorpforeningNybro-
Korpen/Hem/Kubb

laget.se/signalgatan

Switzerland
baselcitykubb.ch

U.S. National Kubb Championship
usakubb.org

Wisconsin
wisconsinkubb.com
foxvalleykubb.net

World Championship of Kubb
vmkubb.com

Purchase Tournament Quality Kubb Sets from:

Aaron Ellringer's Kubb Farm
kubbfarm.com

JP's Backyard Games
jpsbackyardgames.yolasite.com

Appendix III.
Introduction to the Planet Kubb Game Notation

It's game two of the 2012 US National Kubb Championship's quarterfinals - Knockerheads v. Tad Kubbler. The Knockerheads' Josh Feathers prepares to throw in nine kubbs. If Josh and the Knockerheads win this, they move forward to the semifinals.

Nine field kubbs and six batons. Will the Knockerheads leave Tad Kubbler an advantage line? And if they do—is their championship quest over?

With the Planet Kubb Game Notation it is now possible to start to answer these questions. Just as baseball has the all-telling box score, Kubb now has a simple, fast and effective, method of transcribing and archiving Kubb games for easy sharing and statistical analysis.

The Game Notation was developed by Jamie Thingelstad

and Garrick van Buren early in 2012 as a simple way to describe each turn within a Kubb game. It debuted at the 2012 US Championship after being tested on several kubb games on YouTube as well as field tested in actual game play. The Notation can be learned in a minute and it provides an easy guide to any Kubb game: a 'B' means a baseline kubb was hit, an 'F' means a field kubb was hit, and a 'K' means the king was slain.

With this we can describe a perfect kubb game as follows:

B   B   B   B   B   K

One 'B' or baseline kubb hit by each of the first 5 batons with the final baton slaying the king – 'K'.

We can even introduce a letter for each player, to denote who threw each baton. Take this team with players; Josh – 'j', Grant -'g', Dwayne – 'd':

j : B   j : B   g : B   g : B   d : B   d : K

Of course, a kubb game is made of more than baseline kubb hits and king shots. There's missed shots, advantage lines, and throwing kubbs in. The Notation can capture all aspects of a kubb game and has been used to record nearly 100 tournament games worldwide already—including the quarterfinals bracket from the 2012 US Nationals.

Let's return to the quarterfinals game where Josh Feathers is about to throw in nine kubbs. After analyzing the notation of each turns in the recorded games, we know there's a 48% chance one of those nine kubbs will remain—leaving an advantage line for the opponent. Additionally, there's an 85% chance the opponent will immediately convert that advantage line into a win.

How do the Knockerheads perform?

Let's take a look:

j:9i3r   j:5F   j:2F   g:F   g:-   d:-   d:F

Josh throws in nine kubbs, and had to re-throw three (j:9i3r).
Then with the very first baton he knocks down five field
kubbs (j:5f), then two more with the second baton (j:2F).
Grant then takes care of one more field kubb (g:F), misses
(g:-) and steps back for Dwayne. Dwayne also misses (d:-)
risking the odds before toppling the final field kubb (d:F).

Tad Kubbler is now up with Eric Goplin ('e') throwing in nine
kubbs, after four re-throws.

e : 9I4R   c : 3F   c : -   a : 3F   a : F   e : -   e : -

Cole ('c') immediately topples three field kubbs (c:3F)
followed by a miss (c:-). Anders ('a') also hits a triple (a:3F)
and a single (a:F). Unfortunately, Eric misses twice leaving an
advantage line—just as the statistics predicted would
happen with nine field kubbs.

Also just as the statistics predicted, the Knockerheads
immediately win.

j : 7IR A   j : 5F   j : F   g : F   d : K   X   X

Josh now only throws in seven (and only one re-throw). Then
he moves up to the advantage line (A) and topples 5 (j:5F)
followed by a single (j:F). Grant finishes the last field kubb
(g:F) then steps back while Dwayne slays the king (d:K). The
Knockerheads move into the semifinals with two unthrown
batons (X).

This quarterfinal game between Knockerheads and Tad
Kubbler had 20 turns. Across those 20 turns, the
Knockerheads hit wood 62% of the time compared to Tad
Kubbler's 60%. This tells us that these two teams are very

evenly matched and both hold up well to the stresses of tournament-level play.

The notation isn't just to tournament play. It's easy enough to remember and quick enough to jot down during friendlies or practices to gauge your own skill level and track improvements.

The downloadable Planet Kubb Scoresheet includes the most used notation and supports a 20 turn game. Once the data is on the scoresheet (or even if it's not), everyone is welcome to enter their game statistics into the Planet Kubb Wiki. This will automatically calculate hit percentages for the game, each player, and feed into the overall Kubb game statistics.

Additionally, Kubb players have started scoring games from tournaments (both in person and using YouTube videos) making it possible for us to understand both individual performances, team strengths and overall game dynamics. When game video is available—as it is for this Knockerheads v. Tad Kubbler game—the video is embedded into the Planet Kubb game page. This makes it easy to follow along as the game unfolds and revise the game's notation as needed.

The Planet Kubb Game Notation is a tremendously exciting innovation for the sport of Kubb. It provides a statistical framework for understanding this simple, yet complex game. It adds the best of chess notation, the excitement of sports statistics and allows kubb teams to compare their play across time, languages and countries!

Appendix IV.
Planet Kubb Game
Notation Primer

Kubb Tossing Phase

I   number of kubbs thrown in.

R   number of kubbs re-thrown because they landed out of bounds.

P   number of penalty kubbs thrown (kubbs thrown out of bounds twice).

Advantage Line

A   indicates the team is throwing from an advantage line. Prepended number indicated estimated distance (in meters) of advantage.

Baton Tossing Phase

- (dash)   baton did not knock anything down.
B   base kubbs hit.
F   number of field kubbs hit, prepended number indicates multiples.
K   king hit
=   king miss
X   unthrown baton

For the full and current notation visit wiki.planetkubb.com/wiki/Notation

Appendix V.
The Simplest Mindful Meditation

1. Sit quietly.

2. Imagine your inhale and exhale are a circle.

3. Allow your mind to wander.

4. Acknowledge and gently return focus to your breath.

5. Repeat. Unexpected thoughts will arise. Let them. Gently return your focus to your breath and they will pass. Let them.

6. When you are done, acknowledge the quiet around you. Then arise.

GARRICK VAN BUREN

About the Author

Garrick van Buren was introduced to kubb in 2011. Like so many others—he immediately fell in love with the game. Off the kubb pitch, he's an expert in internet-based software products and the teams that build them. Garrick frequently speaks on the topic of technology and life balance. He lives in suburban Minneapolis with his wife and four children.